William Henry Egle, Thomas Hastings Robinson

Addresses delivered before the Dauphin County Historical Society

In the state capitol, Harrisburg, July 4, 1876

William Henry Egle, Thomas Hastings Robinson

Addresses delivered before the Dauphin County Historical Society
In the state capitol, Harrisburg, July 4, 1876

ISBN/EAN: 9783337137434

Printed in Europe, USA, Canada, Australia, Japan

Cover: Foto ©Andreas Hilbeck / pixelio.de

More available books at **www.hansebooks.com**

ADDRESSES

DELIVERED BEFORE THE

DAUPHIN COUNTY HISTORICAL SOCIETY

IN THE

STATE CAPITOL,

HARRISBURG,

JULY 4, 1876.

ECCLESIASTICAL HISTORY

—OF—

DAUPHIN COUNTY,

—BY—

THOMAS H. ROBINSON, D. D.

DAUPHIN COUNTY IN HISTORY.

[In every section of Dauphin county, the one hundredth anniversary of American Independence was celebrated with a degree of enthusiasm scarcely equaled since Independence Bell "Proclaimed Liberty throughout all the Land," in 1776. In the City of Harrisburg, and the boroughs of Lykens, Millersburg and Middletown, the celebration embraced civic parades, orations, and displays of fire-works. At the seat of government the arrangements for addresses to be delivered on the occasion, was conceded, as it was confided to the Historical Society of Dauphin county, which at once directed the preparation of appropriate sketches, assigned as follows:

The Ecclesiastical History of Dauphin County:
To Rev. Thomas H. Robinson, D. D.

Dauphin County in the Revolution:
To A. Boyd Hamilton.

Historical Review of Dauphin County:
To William H. Egle, M. D.

In addition to these, John L. Sexton was requested to prepare an address on the "Industrial Progress of Pennsylvania." The three former being the more intimately connected with the historic record of the county of Dauphin, are herewith presented.

The parade of the Fourth of July was gotten up under
the auspices of the Order of Odd Fellows and the Fire
Department of the City, and was exceedingly creditable
to their taste, energy and patriotism. At the conclusion
of the parade a large audience had assembled in the Hall
of the House of Representatives, animated with the joy-
ous memory of the One Hundredth Anniversary of the
Signing of the Declaration of Independence. No more
pleasant concourse of patriotic citizens was gathered in
any part of the Union, than the one beneath the dome of
the Capitol of the great Commonwealth of Pennsylvania.
The meeting was called to order by A. BOYD HAMILTON,
Esq., President of the Dauphin County Historical Society. The Rev. JOEL SWARTZ, D. D., of the First Lutheran
Church, delivered a fervent prayer appropriate to the
occasion, when SAMUEL D. INGRAM, Esq., read the immor-
tal document, the anniversary of whose signing was that
day commemorated throughout the length and breadth of
the United States. After which the Historical addresses
following were delivered.]

THE ECCLESIASTICAL HISTORY OF DAU-
PHIN COUNTY.

BY THOMAS H. ROBINSON, D. D.

One hundred years ago the civilized settlements of our
country were mainly confined to a narrow strip of territory along the Atlantic coast. The traveler who ventured
from the seaside soon found himself approaching the
boundaries of the white population. Civilization had only
brightened the eastern edges of our great land, and

kindled a fire here and there in the deeper forests. This region of the Susquehanna was, at the time of the revolution, on the frontier. Through the district of the Cumberland valley, now filled with a population of about two hundred and fifty thousand, there was then a scattered people not exceeding forty thousand in number.

A few settlements had been made up the Susquehanna and along its north and west branches, the region of the Juniata was opened, and some settlers had crossed the Alleghenies on their pack horses, and built their homes in the western part of the State. As early indeed as 1720, traders and settlers were pushing their way out into the grand forests along our noble river, and when the war of the revolution began there were men enough who sprung to arms, to form some of the bravest regiments of the times. But the country was still primitive, and the type of manners and customs of education and religion, partook of the characteristics of an early time and a hardy race. Dauphin county had not yet been organized but was included in Lancaster.

The man who seeks to comprehend the history of this country or any section of it, should know that the American people at their birth were emphatically a *religious people*. It was largely for religion and its rights that they braved the seas and came hither to plant their new government in this western world. They were not adventurers seeking the excitements of a strange land, or speculators in search of an El Dorado of gold. They wanted to serve God freely and intelligently, and scarcely, therefore, was the humble cabin of the original settler erected, before the school house and the church were built. Education and Christianity were among the first necessities.

Throughout this entire region, from the Alleghenies eastward to the Susquehanna, and still eastward to the line of the counties adjoining our own, the bulk of the earliest settlers were of that class now familiarly known as the Scotch-Irish. This people took to the frontiers, and in the Indian wars stood as a bulwark of protection for the eastern part of the colony. It has only been in later years that they have been gradually and peaceably displaced by the sturdy and solid Germans.

It so happened, therefore, from the race of people who settled here, that the first churches organized within the limits of Dauphin county were Calvinistic. They were

THE PRESBYTERIAN CHURCHES OF DERRY, PAXTON AND HANOVER.

These all date back prior to the year 1730, although Hanover had no settled pastor until 1738, when the Rev. Richard Sanckey was settled over the church. The first pastor of the united churches of Derry and Paxton was the Rev. William Bertram, who took charge of them in 1732. Prior to this last date the people of this region were dependent for the preaching of the gospel upon the ministers of the churches in the region further eastward. For fully one hundred and twenty years these three old churches of Derry, Paxton and Hanover flourished in their strength, filling up an eventful and honorable history. The old Derry church has the honor of being the pioneer church of the county. The venerable building, constructed of oak logs two feet thick and covered with hemlock boards on the outside, is still standing. It was erected as early as 1720. The congregation that worshiped in it lies buried in the ivy grown graveyard by its side or in others in distant parts of the land. But one of the three early churches now survives—Paxton.

The original settlers and their children are gone, and the churches of other denominations occupy the ground. The first Presbyterian organization within the limits of Harrisburg was in 1794, and the first settled pastor was the Rev. Nathaniel R. Snowden. At a very early date there was a Presbyterian church in Upper Paxton. Its building stood on the hill back of the village of Dauphin. The leading ministers of the Presbyterian church in this county in the past were the Revs. John Elder, John Roan, Richard Sanckey and William R. DeWitt, D. D. There are now in the county eight churches of the Presbyterian order, with two or three mission stations. Five of these churches are in the city of Harrisburg. There is now a church membership in the Presbyterian churches of the county of about 1,400, a Sunday school membership of 2,500, sittings in their churches for about 3,500 people. Their Sunday schools number 10.

THE REFORMED CHURCH.

The Reformed church was second in date of organization, a church having been started in Derry in the year 1768. Soon after the laying out of the town of Harrisburg in the year 1785, the settlers who were composed of several denominations, took measures to build a church, and when it was built in 1787, clergymen of different denominations, by permission, officiated in it. The building was, however, owned an occupied regularly by the German Reformed and Lutheran congregations. These two bodies used it jointly, each, however, electing their own church officers, trustees, elders and deacons.

In 1795 the two churches separated, but continued their worship in the same building, until the year 1814.

The building became the exclusive property of the Reformed church in 1816. It was the first church building erected in Harrisburg, and stood on the corner of Third street and Cherry alley, near the Salem Reformed church of the present day. Prior to 1786 the early settlers of Harrisburg held divine worship in a one story log school house which stood at the foot of capitol hill, on the north corner of Third and Walnut streets, which is still standing on the south side of Walnut street, between sixth and Canal.

The Rev. Anthony Hautz, of the Reformed church was the first settled pastor within the limits of Harrisburg, being here from about 1790 to 1797. Eleven pastors have succeeded him in the care of the church, among them the two Helfensteins, Rev. Dr. Zacharias, Rev. Dr. J. F. Mesick and Rev. David Gans. The Reformed church has grown rapidly since that early day, and has now organizations in nearly every township and district of the county, having according to some late statement, about thirty church organizations and preaching stations, and a seating capacity in their church edifices for nearly 14,000 people.

THE LUTHERAN CHURCH.

The Lutheran church was the third in date of organization in the county, having begun an enterprise in Hummelstown as early as 1753. In 1787, as already stated, the Lutherans of the town of Harrisburg united with the members of the Reformed church in erecting and occupying the first church building in our present city limits. In 1814 they withdrew and purchased a lot on Fourth street and erected a church edifice of their own, and beside it a large two-story brick school house.

Their first pastor was the Rev. F. D. Schaeffer, who began to preach in and around Harrisburg in 1788.

Their first stationed pastor was the Rev. Henry Mueller, who began his labors in 1795. He has been succeeded by a number of earnest and able men, among whom may be named the Lochmans, Rev. Dr. C. W. Schaeffer, Rev. Dr. C. A. Hay and Rev. Dr. G. F. Stelling. The Lutheran church is progressing rapidly in the county. New churches are being erected; its membership increases; its Sunday schools are large and flourishing. According to a late report there are now thirty-six organizations in the county, and room in its church edifices for over ten thousand people.

The three bodies, the Presbyterian, the Reformed and the Lutheran seem to have been the only religious bodies that had any position and regularly organized existence in the county prior to the year 1800.

THE METHODIST EPISCOPAL CHURCH.

In the summer of 1801 the Rev. William Rose, an Irishman, organized some classes and preaching appointments for the M. E. Church in the upper end of the county, one at Halifax, another at Millersburg, and a third up Lykens Valley. Here began the Methodism of the county. The first Methodist families in the county are said to have been residents of Halifax. Harrisburg became, however, a preaching station as early a 1802.

The Rev. Jacob Gruber, was appointed on the circuit as early as 1802 and preached at this point. The first society formed in Harrisburg was in 1810. The present fine edifice on State street is the outgrowth of the feeble band of 1802. With characteristic zeal and energy this church has pushed its conquests until to-day; it has nearly or quite 25 organizations in the county, a church membership of probably 2,500 to 3,000, about 4,000 children in its Sunday schools, and churches that will seat 6,000 people.

THE PROTESTANT EPISCOPAL CHURCH.

As early as 1766, this church had a mission station at Estherton, two miles above Harrisburg, as a few families of that church were residing there, but no church building was erected. It was not until 1826 that a congregation was formed in the county, the present St. Stephen's church of this city. The congregation worshiped for a time in the building already mentioned, on the corner of Third street and Cherry alley, which was built by the people of the Reformed and Lutheran church. The first rector of the church was the Rev. Mr. Clemson. Among his successors have been those who were greatly honored in this community. The number of church organizations in the county at this date is five.

THE ROMAN CATHOLIC CHURCH.

The first congregation organized of this church in the county was within the present limits of the city of Harrisburg. As early, however, as 1810, the ground now owned by them on Allison's Hill was in their possession, and the Jesuit Fathers visited the place and had ministrations. There also was their first graveyard. At a later date the property came into the hands of William Allison, but in subsequent years was re-acquired by the Catholics, and is now held by them. The first church edifice erected by them was begun in 1826, under the superintendence of the Rev. Michael Curran. It was the original of the present pro-Cathedral on State street.

The Rev. P. Maher was for nearly 35 years the officiating minister of this church, and will be kindly remembered by persons of all denominations. The present bishopric was formed in 1868. The church is in a flourishing state, having a large membership and an excellent Sunday school. There are several other organizations of this church in the city and county.

THE BETHEL, OR "CHURCH OF GOD."

This religious body originated in this county. Its founder was the Rev. John Winebrenner, who withdrew from the Reformed Church and began a new organization in 1827. Their first church building was erected in Mulberry street between Front and Second streets, occupying the grounds where now stands the city hospital. This church has pushed its work vigorously, and now claims some fifteen or sixteen organizations in the county. Its energy in the work of Sunday schools is worthy of all praise.

BAPTIST AND FREE BAPTIST CHURCHES.

The Baptist church made its first organization on the 2d of April, 1830, in a building known as the Unitarian Church, which has since passed out of existence with the people that built it. The Rev. Dyer A. Nichols was the first pastor of the enterprise. There are at present several organizations in the county of the Baptist order, about a dozen. Their churches would accommodate about 3,000 hearers.

During the last half century several other Protestant denominations have formed churches in the city and county and are pushing forward their Christian work with great devotion and success. Among them may be

2

mentioned the United Brethren, whose first organization in Dauphin county was about 1800. They have now 38 churches, about 2400 church members; Sunday schools with a membership of 2700 scholars and teachers. The Evangelical Association, organized about the same time; the Wesley Union church about the year 1830.

Our Jewish brethren have also their synagogues, the first of which was formed about 1854.

How great the contrast between those early days, and these would take longer time to depict than is alloted me to-day. In 1776 this district, now Dauphin county, had within its borders about 10,000 inhabitants. To-day it has fully 70,000. In 1776 Harrisburg was but a trading post, to-day it is a city of nearly 30,000. In 1776 there were three strong country churches—Derry, Paxton and Hanover, and a few other preaching stations. To-day we have in this city alone over forty churches, and in the county between one hundred and fifty and two hundred.

Moved by a generous rivalry and working in the spirit of noble harmony, these Christian Churches have gone forth to possess every part of our county and to carry the gospel with its light and salvation to every home. Not only has this Christian civilization filled our city and surrounding villages, and dotted over the whole county with these houses of holy worship, but it has given us all other needed benevolent institutions. The religious bodies, Protestant and Catholic, have kept pace with the increasing population and have anticipated it in providing the means and the places for religious culture.

Great as has been the progress of population in the country from the year 1776 to the present, it has been far outstripped by the growth of the churches. In 1776 there were less than 1,950 evangelical churches in the

United States; according to the census of 1870 there
were then over 72,000. The population in a century increased only thirteen fold, the churches increased over
thirty-six fold. In 1790 there was one evangelical minister for every 2,000 of the people, while now there is
one for about every 700. In 1790 there were five members of evangelical churches for every 100 of population; there are now eighteen for every 100.

In 1776 there were no Bible, tract or missionary societies; not a single religious newspaper published in the
land, nor any house for the publication of religious liter-
ature, nor even the publication of religious books to any
extent. Our orphan asylums, schools of reform, Christian associations, temperance societies, etc., etc., etc., are
all of later date. Truly, the Church of God moves onward.

There are but few districts in our great country that
are better provided than our own county with the varied
advantages of intellectual and religious culture. Our
churches are multiplying. The great body of our people are law-abiding, upright and moral. The Sabbath
Bible, the Church and the agencies of Christianity are
honored among us.

When we look back one hundred years and more to
the days of our fathers and of the early pioneers of this
region, how changed the aspect. The victories of peace
have long ago effaced the sad memorials of a war that
filled many a lowly cabin with horror. The banks of
this broad and placid stream, where once rang the war-
whoop of the savage, and where broken families gathered in groups to mourn over their slaughtered dead, now
smile with orchards and teeming harvests and gardens,
with workshops, and villages, and happy homes.

Here, where once was carnage, no sounds prevail but the hum of industry, of peaceful life and joy. When we look upon this beautiful region with its streams and mountains, its cultivated farms, its railroads and manufactories, its flourishing towns and villages, its institutions of learning and of charity, its multiplied and stately church edifices, and all the indications of the social, intellectual and moral condition of its people, and recall that just one hundred years ago our fathers, clad in their linsey woolsey or in their buckskin, with their powder horns at their side and their flint-lock muskets, were pouring forth to join the army of the Revolution, going forth from the lowly homes where they had prayed, and the churches where they had worshiped to fight in a cause that no men understood better than did they, we ask ourselves anew, Do we not owe a debt of grateful memory to them, and of largest thanksgiving to God, for the lives they lived and the work they did for us and for our children after us ? Let us not stint our gratitude to the men who planted in the wilderness homes where intelligence and enterprise and religion were all nourished.

They were men who spared no cost in preparing the way for more peaceful and happy times. Let us not think lightly of the men who opened out these unbroken forests, who broke up the virgin soil of these valleys, who reared cabins for Christian households, who taught their sons to love freedom, to contend for the right and revere the God of their fathers. They were no ordinary men, they brought here the spirit of liberty fresh and warm in their hearts.

They sought to lay deep and broad the foundation for righteous ages after them. They learned their political creed as they learned their religion, from the Bible—that

Bible which says, "The truth shall make you free." And nearly every man of them who was able to bear arms and endure a soldier's life, entered into the service of his country. And two years before the Declaration of Independence was proclaimed, the men of this county assembled June 4, 1774, at Hanover, and among other resolutions, passed the following:

"*Resolved*, That in the event of Great Britain attempting to force unjust laws upon us by strength of arms, our cause we leave to heaven and our rifles."

We are living in the past to-day. We are recalling the eventful times, the thrilling adventures, the heroic endurance, the toils and self denials, the services and the virtues of our fathers. And we rightly say this large, rich present is not what *we* have made it. These things around us are *their* achievement. But now what is to be the practical outcome of all that we have, and learn and feel to-day? What good is it to have had such fathers if we to-day are not worthy of them?

What glory to us to look back into such a radiant past, if we are going to mar all the picture by not imitating them and carrying on their work? If they who had so little, did so much for truth, for country, for us and for God, what shall be the measure of our doing who are so rich and strong?

Our opportunity of doing good and blessing men are to theirs as our railroads to the Indian trails and mountain bridle paths; as the electric telegraph to the old stage coach; as the modern mower and reaper to the old fashioned scythe; as the steam engine to the slow moving water wheel; as the mighty trip hammers of our steel works to the light blows of some village blacksmith.

The voices of the past summon us to duty. The men who founded school and church within the sound of the Indians' war-whoop, charge us to make the future as much greater and fairer than the present, as the present is richer and greater in all the achievements of art, and the blessings of freedom and religion, than the past.

THE REVOLUTIONARY SOLDIERS

OF

DAUPHIN COUNTY,

·

BY

A. BOYD HAMILTON.

Mr. A. Boyd Hamilton, of Harrisburg, then delivered the following address:

HEROES AND PATRIOTS OF DAUPHIN COUNTY ONE HUNDRED YEARS AGO.

Upon an occasion such as this, it is fitting that the present should show its appreciative gratitude to those whose records form a glorious past. It is the province of history to preserve from oblivion recollections of deeds whose character made a name and nation.

With these objects in view, this brief account is prepared, recalling the memories of those who laid lives and fortunes upon the altar of their country, and who contributed to an uncommon extent personal effort as their share to secure that independence, to celebrate which has caused us to assemble this day.

The present Dauphin, then part of Lancaster county, presents a remarkable roll of honor, from 1775, when the revolution commenced, to its conclusion in 1783. It comprises of officers alone about 150, and of privates nearly 2,000 persons. This exceeds in magnitude any contribution made since that period, from any part of Pennsylvania to the military service of the country. It suggests a train of thought very gratifying to those whose ancestry formed a part of this patriotic band. When it is remembered that these soldiers were drawn from a sparse population along the borders of the Susquehanna river, the Swatara, Beaver, Manada and Wiconisco creeks, the aggregate is most surprising.

These people were engaged at that time, in preparing rugged forests for future cultivation, in the labor common to a frontier life, yet old and young seem to have cheerfully forsaken all to follow the fortunes of "a nation that had as yet no flag." This day there are more than a million "starry banners" floating in this single county.

No sooner was a call for volunteers issued in 1775, than we find a company formed in Paxton and Derry to march "for Boston," soon after to Quebec, having as officers and privates Matthew Smith, James Crouch, Richard Dixon, Archibald Steele, Michael Simpson, John Joseph Henry, John and David Harris, sons of Harris, founder of Harrisburg, and other honored names, now seldom recalled, but the remembrance of whose valiant deeds, hardy endurance, and patriotic sacrifices should never be forgotten by a grateful people.

The sergeant, Dixon, of "Dixon Ford," on the Swatara, and John Harris, Harris Ferry, never returned from the campaign to and assault on Quebec. One of them, certainly, was killed there—the exact fate of the latter is quite uncertain. Alexander Nelson of Derry was also killed in this assault.*

---

*NOTE.—It has been a work of patience and research to recover so much of the roll of Smith's brave men as is herewith presented. It is thought all that marched from the present Dauphin county are embraced in it. I do not think it possible to recover a complete list of the company. It was 87 strong, and all of them from the then, Lancaster county. This roll names 48 of them. Who were the other 39? No papers of Smith, Steel, Simpson or Cross, are known. Indeed almost all we know of that celebrated event, or of the heroic men who formed its ranks, is found in the memoir of it by Judge Henry—a *private* soldier.

Lieutenant Michael Simpson commanded, under an order of Gen. Arnold, the company in the assault on Quebec. Captain Smith was sick at Isle Orleans. An excellent memoir of Gen. Simpson, prepared by George W. Harris, Esq., has been published since the foregoing address was delivered.

OFFICERS AND PRIVATES.

Captain—Matthew Smith, Paxton.
1st Lieut.—Archibald Steel, Donegal.
2d Lieut.—Michael Simpson, Paxton, commanded in the assault.
3d Lieut.—William Cross, Hanover.
Boyd, Thomas, Sergeant, Derry, afterwards Captain-Lieutenant 1st P. M.

It will be impossible in the brief compass to which this must be confined, to do more than refer to the services of those who were subsequently soldiers, afterward, honored and useful citizens of Dauphin county. A recital of the names of most of them is all that can possibly be presented.

Of the considerable number of active officers resident in our own and the present Lebanon county, after 1785, the year of the formation of Dauphin county, very little is known of themselves or families. The memories of the brave privates it is impossible to recover. The feverish migrations previous to 1820 and of several subse-

Binnagle, Curtis, Londonderry.

Bollinger, Emanuel, resided in Dauphin county in 1813.

Black, James, Hanover.

Black, John, Upper Paxton.

Cavenaugh, Edward, resided in York county. "Honest Ned," of Judge Henry.

Carbach, Peter, enlisted in J. P. Scott's Co. March 12, 1777, afterwards in Capt. Selin's, discharged at Lancaster in 1783. Resided in Dearborn county, Indiana, in 1830.

Conner, Timothy, Bethel.

Crouch, James, Paxton, afterwards a Colonel.

Cochran, Samuel, Paxton, afterwards a Captain of militia 1781.

Crow, Henry, died in Derry.

Cunningham, Robert, Londonderry, died at Lancaster of disease contracted in prison, soon after his return.

Dougherty, James, Londonderry, captured at Quebec, and put in irons eight weeks. Enlisted afterwards in 12th Penn.

Dixon, Robert, Sergeant, killed in front of Quebec, Nov. 17, 1775. Belonged to West Hanover.

Dixon, Richard, Dixon's Ford.

Dean, Samuel, served one year, then appointed Lieutenant in Col. Hart's regiment, Flying camp. Subsequently 1st Lieutenant 11th Pa.

Adam Egle, wagon-master at Cambridge, Col. Thompson's regiment. Was in Smith's recruits, from Lebanon township.

Feely, Timothy, Dixon Ford.

Griffith John, Harris Ferry.

Harris, John, Harris Ferry, killed at Quebec.

Harris, David, Harris Ferry.

Henry, John Joseph, Lancaster, died at Harrisburg.

quent years, dispersed families in localities distant from each other. The loss of home scattered their records and weakened their family ties. Indifference to ancestry, to private position, or public affairs seems to have characterized the emigrants from this charming region, to a land supposed to be more fruitful still, beyond the Allegheny mountains. All are aware that the life of a border settler is not conducive to the preservation of records, or of placing in indestructible form accounts of current affairs; and thus it has happened that many things this generation would like to know, are buried so deep in the abyss of oblivion, that it will be the merest accident, if they are ever rescued. Perhaps the imperfect information I pre-

Kennedy John, Hanover.

Marshall, Lawrence, Hanover.

McGranaghan Charles, Londonderry.

Merchant, George, Donegal.

McEnally, Henry, Londonderry.

McKonkey, John, Hanover.

Mellen, Atchison, resided in Lycoming county in 1813.

Nilson, Alexander, Derry, killed in front of Quebec, Jan. 1, 1776.

Old, James, Derry.

Porterfield, Charles, Hanover.

Ryan, John, Derry.

Simpson, William, Paxton, wounded August 27, 1775, brother of Gen. Michael Simpson.

Sparrow, William, Derry.

Shaeffer, John, drummer, resided in Lancaster in 1809.

Smith, Samuel, Paxton.

Taylor, Henry, captured 31st December, 1775; returned 10th November, 1776.

Tidd, [Todd,] John, of Hanover.

Teeder, Michael, re-enlisted in 5th Penn.

Warner, James, died in the wilderness near Chaudiere lake.—Henry, p. 198.

Wheeler. ———, [uncertain, from Paxton.]

Weirick, Valentine, Hanover, resided in Dauphin county in 1813.

Waun, Michael, Derry.

Nilson [Nelson probably] and Waun did not return. The former was killed in the assault. The other died at the "crossing of the Chaudiere." Thus Dixon, Harris and Nilson were killed in the battle.

sent is as complete a record as can be gathered at this date, and is the only statement in a permanent form that has ever been collected. If for no other, this is a good reason for its preservation. In only one or two instances, has it appeared that the evils of ignorance, poverty, or vice, have overtaken any of the race of these noble fathers.

With these preliminary observations, the subject will be taken up based upon a list of names prepared by and contained in a circular issued by the Dauphin County Historical Society in May last, and with such other information as has since come to the knowledge of that organization.

A great majority of those who served from Paxton, Derry, Hanover, Upper Paxton and Londonderry, the townships into which the upper part of Lancaster county was divided in 1774, were styled "associators," officered by those of their own choice, and serving short terms of duty as called upon by the supreme executive council. Many of them as early as the first year of the contest, entered the Pennsylvania line composed of thirteen regiments, enlisted for a term of three years. Whenever it has been possible to separate those who served as associators from those who were continental officers, it has been done.

In a few instances, company rolls have been recovered, but all search has been ineffectual in securing any number of them. We know that Boyd, Wallace, Morrison Hays, McKnight, Wilson, McKee, Armstrong, McClure, Fleming, Bennet, Cochran, and other familiar names marched with Col. Timothy Greene, whilst Forster, Rutherford, Harris, Carson, Elder, Gray, McElhenny, Crawford, Gilchrist, Montgomery, McFarlane, Espy, and so on, marched under Cowden, Murray or Crouch. Happily the information respecting the following who in 1776, or afterwards, citizens of Dauphin county is precise, and authentic as to dates and services.

Matthew Smith, June 25, 1775, captain in Col. William Thompson's Rifle regiment, which afterwards became the 1st Pennsylvania of the line, Col. Hand; promoted major in 9th Pennsylvania December 1, 1776; Vice President Executive Council, October 11, 1779; prothonotary of Northumberland county, Feb. 4, 1780–83. Died at Milton, 1794; buried at Warrior's Run.

Archibald Steel, 1st lieutenant in Smith's company June 25, 1775; wounded at Quebec, losing two fingers; captured December 31, 1775; carried on the rolls as lieutenant of 1st Pennsylvania. In service 57 years. Dying commander of the Frankford arsenal, aged 97, October 19, 1832. Buried at Philadelphia.

Michael Simpson, 2d lieutenant in Smith's company June 25, 1775; promoted captain of 1st Pennsylvania December 1, 1776; relieved from service January 1, 1781. Died June 1, 1813. Buried at Paxton, aged 65 years.

William Cross, 2d lieutenant in Col. Moylan's cavalry regiment; July 3, 1777, promoted captain 4th Pennsylvania regiment. Buried at Hanover, Dauphin county.

John Joseph Henry, private in Smith's company. (See his memoirs.) Died April 15, 1811.

John Hamilton, captain of volunteer unattached cavalry, December, 1776; marched to the relief of Washington before the battle of Trenton; again called out in 1778. Died and is buried at Harrisburg 1793, aged 43 years.

Alexander Graydon, captured January 5, 1776; 3d Pennsylvania battalion, Col. Shee; taken November 16,

1776, at Fort Washington; exchanged April 15, 1778. Died at Philadelphia, May 2, 1818, aged 67. (See his memoir.)

John Harris, commissioned captain of 12th Pennsylvania, Col. Wm. Cook, October 14, 1776. Founder of Harrisburg. Died July 29, 1791. Buried at Paxton, aged 65 years.

Dr. Robert Harris, Nov. 1, 1777, commissioned surgeon's mate of 2d Pennsylvania regiment of the line. Died March 4, 1785, at Blue Ball tavern, Tredyfferin township, in Chester county, of an attack of quinsy, on his way from Philadelphia.

James Crouch died an aged man, at Walnut Hill, near Middletown, May 24, 1794; had been at Quebec, Princeton, Monmouth, Germantown, and rose from a private at Quebec, to be colonel of one of the Pennsylvania regiments. He is buried at Paxton.

John Stoner, appointed lieutenant of Capt. John Murray's company, Col. Miles' regiment, March 15, 1776; promoted captain 10th Pennsylvania regiment, December 4, 1776. Died at Harrisburg March 24, 1825, aged 77.

Andrew Lee, died June 30, 1821, aged 80 years. Native of Paxton. Buried at Hanover, Luzerne county.

Ambrose Crain enlisted as a private in Capt. John Marshall's company, Col. Miles' regiment; promoted quartermaster sergeant July 15, 1776, and in April, 1777, second Lieutenant of Capt. Anderson's company, Col. Stewart's 10th Pennsylvania. Buried at Hanover.

Adam Boyd, second lieutenant on the armed ship Burke, Jan. 23, 1776; promoted to first lieutenant October 4, 1776; honorably discharged July 16, 1777; lieutenant in the Northampton county contingent August,

1777, at Brandywine, Germantown to Yorktown. Died May, 1814, aged 68 years, and is buried at Harrisburg.

John Murray, captain, Col. Miles' regiment, March 7, 1776; promoted major April 18, 1777; lieutenant colonel of 2d Pennsylvania regiment in 1780; relieved from service January 1, 1781; died in Chillisquaque township, Northumberland county. His company was from Upper Paxton and nearly used up at Long Island December 27, 1776.

Andrew Forrest, second lieutenant Captain Graydon's company, 3d Pennsylvania battery; captured November 16, 1776, at Fort Washington; exchanged October 25, 1780. A physician and long resident of Harrisburg. Died at Danville 1815.

Captain John Brisban, commissioned January 5, 1776, 2d Pennsylvania battery, Col. Arthur St. Clair; served one year, died March 13, 1822, aged 91; buried at Paxton.

David Harris, second son of John the founder, was an officer early in the contest—rose to be a major, removed to and died at Baltimore.

Capt. John Marshall's company, Col. Miles' regiment, was raised in Hanover; his lieutenants were John Clark, Thomas Gourley and Stephen Hanna. This fine company was nearly destroyed at the battle of Long Island, August 27, 1776.

Samuel Weir, commissioned second lieutenant 1777, had served at Princeton previously, and was an officer at Germantown and Yorktown. Died 1820, aged 76 years, and buried at Harrisburg.

Archibald McAllister, commissioned second lieutenant July, 1776; served at Monmouth, Princeton to Yorktown. Died at Fort Hunter, an historical spot in the border wars from 1750 to 1768. Died at and is buried at Fort Hunter.

James Cowden, a native of Paxton, Dauphin county; colonel of Associators. Died in the house in which he was born October 10, 1810, aged 73 years. Buried at Paxton church yard.

The law relative to "Associators" was a very strict one. It was provided that an officer so forgetful of his position as to use profane language was held to pay a fine of five shillings for each oath; a private was fined for a like offence one shilling and "further punishment." Thus indulgence in profanity was a costly luxury.

An officer guilty of drunkenness was visited with expulsion and reduction to the ranks; a private fined and "further punishment."

All landlords were forbidden to distress Associators under pain of punishment, the grade of which the councils wisely, as it seems to us, did not name. We have met with no instance of this threat being executed.

Non-associators were compelled to pay a tax, generally of three dollars, twice a year to the State. It was collected with unusual severity.

The patriotism of the "Associators" was encouraged by stirring addresses from the brave and brilliant men who were at the head of the movement—those who were to give enduring form to institutions which exist to this day. One example is given, an eloquent and inspiring appeal to Pennsylvania, from those who assembled in June, 1776, to form a State constitution. No State paper before or during this contest of arms that followed, breathes more lofty sentiments, purer patriotism or intense love of freedom, than this. For these reasons it is quoted at length. It will bear perusal now with as lively admiration as it did one hundred years ago.

4

TO THE ASSOCIATORS OF PENNSYLVANIA.

Gentlemen:—The only design of our meeting together was to put an end to our own power in the Province, by fixing upon a plan for calling for a convention, to form a government under the authority of the people. But the sudden and unexpected separation of the late assembly has compelled us to undertake the execution of a resolve of Congress, for calling forth 4,500 of the militia of the Province, to join the militia of the neighboring Colonies, to form a camp for our immediate protection. We presume only to *recommend* the plan we have formed to you, trusting that in a case of so much consequence, your love of virtue and zeal for liberty, will supply the want of authority delegated to us expressly for that purpose.

We need not remind you that you are now furnished with new motives to animate and support your courage.

You are not about to contend against the power of Great Britain, in order to displace one set of villains to make room for another. Your arms will not be enervated in the day of battle with the reflection, that you are to risk your lives or shed your blood for a British tyrant; or that your posterity will have your work to do over again.

You are about to contend for permanent freedom, to be supported by a government which will be derived from yourselves, and which will have for its object, not the emolument of one man or class of men only, but the safety, liberty and happiness of every individual in the community. We call upon you therefore by the respect and obedience, which are due to the authority of the United Colonies, to concur in this important measure. The present campaign will probably decide the fate of America. It is now in your power to immortalize your names, by mingling your achievements with the events of the year 1776—a year which we hope will be famed in the annals of history to the end of time, for establishing upon a lasting foundation the liberties of one quarter of the globe.

Remember the honor of our colony is at stake. Should you desert the common cause at the present juncture, the glory you have acquired by your former exertions of strength and virtue will be tarnished; and our friends and brethren who are now acquiring laurels in the most remote parts of America, will reproach us and blush to own themselves natives or inhabitants of Pennsylvania.

But there are other motives before you. Your houses, your fields, the legacies of your ancestors, or the dearly bought fruits of your own industry, and your liberty, now urge you to the field. These cannot plead with you in vain, or we might point out to you further your wives, your children, your aged fathers and mothers who now look up to you for aid, and hope for salvation in this day of calamity only from the instrumentality of your swords.

Remember the name of Pennsylvania!—Think of your ancestors and your posterity.

Signed by an unanimous order of the Conference.

THOMAS M'KEAN, *President.*

JUNE 25, 1776.

Powder was scarce and many persons set to making it, under the principal direction of Dr. Robert Harris, of Donegal, afterwards a surgeon in the line. Muskets and their fixtures were still more difficult to obtain; the material and skill, however, was at hand to manufacture them. A large trade was created in their manufacture at Lancaster, and one or two other points in what is at present our territory. Their cost was about nine pounds, or in the currency of that day twenty-five dollars. Judge John Joseph Henry was an apprentice at this handicraft when he ran off to fight against Quebec. He afterwards was the first law judge of Dauphin county.

During the first years of the war letters are preserved addressed to the "Lancaster Committee," from officers of the Association, stating that certain privates about Swa-

tara were gunsmiths—mostly apprentices—and requesting their excuse from "duty." In no case was such a
request declined; often as it proved, to the great mortifi-
cation of the youth whose ambition it was to distinguish
himself as a defender of his country. Judge Henry,
Captain Shearer and Ensign Young, are prominent ex-
amples of this feeling.

The first formal call upon the Associators was in June,
1775, although in January a notice of such intention was
promulgated to the "Lieutenants" of the counties. The
number demanded of Lancaster county was 600 men, of
which Paxton, Derry, Hanover, Upper Paxton and Londonderry were to furnish about one-half. There arose the
usual dispute about rank amongst those who had held
commands in the provincial service. This among the
Paxton boys, was carried on in the fractious fashion of
the race. It ended so far as our relation is concerned,
in the retirement of Col. James Burd, the senior colonel
of the provincial troops, and in turning over his command to Majors Cornelius Cox, of Estherton, and James
Crouch, of Middletown.

These gentlemen had a great deal of trouble, ere they
were able to get their forces in marching condition.
It occupied the attention of Rev. Mr. Elder, still a lieutenant colonel in the provincial service, Capt. Joseph
Shearer, Capt. John Harris, Capt. Robert Elder, afterwards a lieutenant colonel, Lieutentant William Young
and Ensigns Samuel Berryhill, Thomas Forster, Jacob
Snyder and William Steel, the whole of a wearisome
summer, to get these heroes in good humor. However,
they did get to the field of conflict, and no complaint has
ever been heard that they were not valiant, as well as
obedient soldiers.

At one period or other, besides the officers already mentioned, the following served:

COLONELS.

James Cowden,
Timothy Greene,

James Crawford,
James Cronch.

LIEUTENANT COLONELS.

Robert Elder,

Peter Hetericks.

MAJORS.

Cornelius Cox,
John Rogers,
Abram Latschall,
John Gilchrist, Jr.,
Anthony McCreight,

James Stewart, and perhaps others in these grades, the officers of which were continually being changed by Congress or the Council.

CAPTAINS.

James Rogers,
Patrick Hayes,
Jas. McCreight,
John Hartenrider,
Daniel Bradley,
Samuel Cochran,
Michael Brown. Jr.,
William Allen,
George Lauer,
Robert M'Callen.
Jonathan M'Clure,
William M'Clure, Jr.,
William Murray,

Martin Weaver,
Andrew Stewart,
Geo. M'Millen,
Hugh Robertson,
William Johnson,
William Laird,
John Kean, the elder,
Thomas Koppenheffer,
Benjamin Snodgrass,
James Sayer,
Michael Whitley,
Frederick Hummel, founder of the town of Hummelstown.

LIEUTENANTS.

Matthew Gilchrist,
William Hill,
Adam Mark,
Castle Byers,
William Barnett,
John Bakestose,
William Patterson,
John Ryan,
George Clark,
William Montgomery,
John Matthews,
John Chesney,
John Hallebaugh,
Daniel Hoffman,
Joseph Smith,
Thomas Sturgeon,
William M'Millen,

Michael Linnes,
George Clark,
Emanuel Ferree,
Robert M'Kee, Upper Paxton, promoted to a majority 1779,
John Barrett,
John M'Farland,
Jacob Latchsar,
Peter Brighthel,
John Weaver,
Jacob Gibbins,
Robert Martin,
James Wilson, Derry,
Henry M'Cormick,
Balzer Bomgardner,
Andrew Rogers.

ENSIGNS.

John Eversole,
Jacob Pruder,
William Branden,
James Johnson,
Baltzer Stone,
John Brown, Jr.,
Daniel Stover,
William Stewart,
George Taylor,
James Reed,

William Lochrey,
George Treebaugh,
Jonathan Woodside,
Daniel Hoffman,
James Wallace,
Robert Greenley,
Henry Graham.
John Weaver,
Jacob Stein,
George Killinger.

Many of those present who hear or read this, will find an ancestral name among those who form the foregoing patriotic roll of honor. Very complete notices of Col. Greene, and Rev. Mr. Elder are to be found in printed publications, to which you are referred.

Interesting particulars of them could be recited, but the bounds set to this address is limited and all that is left for us to do is to recall the memories of the fragrant past.

Several of the very earliest settlers, lotholders in Harrisburg, 1785, were men of the revolution—lived long enough to see the village of Harris Ferry—four years Louisburg—then Harrisburg—well equipped for its onward progress to a prosperous and populous community. A few moments devoted to them will close this episode, so interesting in the history of a border land before Dauphin county existed.

These men, Alexander Graydon, our first prothonotary; James Sayer, who was at Germantown and Chadd's Ford with Samuel Weir and John Stoner—Adam Boyd, who had served as an officer in the fight at Chadd's Ford, Germantown and Yorktown—Andrew Mitchel who had served four years from Monmouth to Yorktown—John Hamilton, a cavalry officer at Trenton—John Kean, the younger, at Yorktown—Andrew Forrest, an officer who was "in everything," as he expressed it, from Trenton to Yorktown, and Thomas Forster of Paxton.

To the names of these excellent fathers, must be added those of William Graydon, Joseph, Hugh and John Montgomery, Andrew Gregg, William Murray, Jacob Awl, Conrad Bombaugh, John Hoge, Samuel Grimes (Graham,) Wendel Hipsman, George Hoyer, William Glass, William Milham, and perhaps others of whom we are uncertain, all very early residents of Harrisburg having served for long or short periods during the revolution. William Maclay, one of the first United States Senators from Pennsylvania, was a provincial officer and also one in the revolution. Andrew Lee, long a respected citizen, was at Yorktown, with Joshua Elder.

Most of these gentlemen had been officers during the revolutionary contest, and many of them held high military rank after the revolution. Especial pains was taken to secure their experience in the Whisky insurrection, and in the militia organizations of which they were the leading spirits. May we all cherish the boon of freedom they were so instrumental in securing, before they laid

"Mortality's raiment softly aside."

HISTORICAL REVIEW

OF

DAUPHIN COUNTY,

BY

WILLIAM H. EGLE, M. D.

HISTORICAL REVIEW OF DAUPHIN COUNTY.

At what eventful era the footsteps of the white man trod the green sward of this locality there is no certainty, but from the description of Capt. John Smith, of the Virginia Company, who ascended the Susquehanna as far as the Great Falls (Conewago,) there can be no doubt some of his hardy adventurers explored the country as far as the first range of the Kittochtinny hills. At that period (1608,) the brave Susquehannas reigned here—they yielding subsequently to the conquering Iroquois. Finally (1695-8,) the Shawanese, from the Carolinas, driven from thence by the Catawbas, located at the mouths of the different tributaries of the great river, as high up as the Forks of the Susquehanna.

Although, after the founding of Philadelphia, William Penn planned the laying out of a city on the Susquehanna, it is not certain that the Founder, in his several visits to our majestic river, ever came farther north than the Swatara. The first persons to spy out this goodly heritage of ours were French traders, one of whom located at the mouth of Paxtang creek, towards the close of the seventeenth century. Of this individual, Peter Bezalion, little is known, but until the period, when the intrigues of the French and especially the encroachments of Lord Baltimore began to be feared, he acted as chief interpreter at the principal Indian conferences. He subsequently went to the Ohio, as also the other French traders, and after 1725-6 he is lost sight of. At this period there were Indian villages at Conestoga, at Conoy, at the mouth of the Swahadowry (Swatara,) Peshtank (Paxtang,) Conedoguinet, and Calapascink (Yellow Breeches.) The Cartlidges were located at Conestoga, after the removal of the Le Torts, Bezalion at Paxtang, and Chartier at the village opposite, while roving traders supplied the other Indian towns.

It becoming absolutely necessary to license English traders so as to prevent communication with the French on the Ohio, among the first was John Harris, who perchance entered this then lucrative field, the Indian trade, at the suggestion of his most intimate friend, Edward Shippen, Provincial Secretary.

Of the John Harris, who thus located permanently at Harrisburg, and who gave the name to our city, it may not be inappropriate to refer. "He was as honest a man as ever broke bread," was the high eulogium pronounced by Parson Elder, of blessed memory, as he spoke of the pioneer in after years. Born in the county of Yorkshire, England, although of Welsh descent, about the year 1673, he was brought up in the trade of his father, that of a brewer. Leaving his home on reaching his majority, he worked at his calling some time in the city of London, where he joined, a few years afterwards, a company from his native district, who emigrated to Pennsylvania two or three years prior to Penn's second visit to his Province. Watson states that John Harris' "entire capital amounted to only sixteen guineas."

We first hear of him after his arrival in Philadelphia as a contractor for clearing and grading the streets of that ancient village. In 1698 his name is appended to a remonstrance to the Provincial Assembly against the passage of an act disallowing the franchise to all persons owning real estate less in value than fifty pounds. The memorial had its effect, and the objectionable law was repealed. By letters of introduction to Edward Shippen, the first mayor of Philadelphia, that distinguished gentleman became his steadfast friend, and through his influence, no doubt, were secured those favors which induced him eventually to become the first permanent settler in this locality.

In January, 1705, John Harris received his license from the Commissioners of Property, authorizing and allowing him to "seat himself on the Sasquahannah," and "to erect such buildings as are necessary for his trade, and to en close and improve such quantities of land as he shall think fit." At once he set about building a log house near the Ganawese (Conoy) settlement, but the Indians made complaint to the government that it made them "uneasie," desiring to know if they encouraged it. As in numerous instances when the Provincial authorities were taken to task, they disavowed their own acts. Nevertheless, the "trader" continued his avocation, making frequent visits to the Shawanese villages at the Conewago and Swatara. It is doubtful if John Harris came farther west until after the permanent removal of all the French traders.

It was during one of his expeditions that Harris first beheld the beauty and advantages of the location at Paxtang. It was the best fording place on the Susquehanna, and then, as now in these later days, on the great highway between the North and South, the East and the West. Annually the chiefs of the Five Nations went to the Carolinas, where were located their vast hunting grounds, and these, returning with peltries, found need of a trading post. The eye of that hardy pioneer, looking out over the vast expanse of wood, and plain, and river, saw and knew that it was the place for the realization of that fond dream of the founder of Pennsylvania, the great and good Penn—"a city on the Susquehanna." At the period referred to, the lands lying between the Conewago or Lechay Hills, and the Kittochtinny or Blue Mountains, had not been purchased from the Indians. Of course neither John Harris nor the Scotch-Irish settlers could locate except by the right of squatter sovereignty or as licensed traders. As a trader, it could only be with the permission of the Indians.

Harris' first move was the erection of a store-house, which he surrounded by a stockade. It was located on the lower bank of the river, at about what is now the foot of Paxtang street. A well dug by him still exists, although covered over about twenty-five years ago, the old pump stock having become useless and the platform dangerous. A mound or hillock about one hundred feet south-east of the graveyard denotes the spot. "For almost a century," in the language of the present David Harris, "this well supplied a large neighborhood with water, which was exceedingly cool and pleasant to the taste." Adjoining his cabin were sheds for the housing of peltries obtained by traffic, which at stated periods, were conveyed to Philadelphia on pack horses.

About the year 1718 or '19, an incident took place in the life of John Harris which has received all sorts of versions, and even doubts of its truthfulness. We shall give it as we believe it, and as traditionary and other facts in our possession supply the material therefor. All the French traders having "gone over Sasquahannah," John Harris monopolized the business at Paxtang. In glancing over the records of the Province of Pennsylvania, frequent allusions are made to the excursions of the northern Indians, either to hunting grounds in the South or to a conflict with a deadly foe. At one time the Onondagoes, on a predatory excursion against the Talapoosas, in Virginia, descending the Susquehanna, left their canoes at Harris', proceeding thence to the scene of strife. Situated as he was, at the best ford on the river, he commanded an extensive trade. His Indian neighbors (Shawanese) were very friendly, and of course would not allow any strange or predatory bands to molest him. The deadly foe of the red race is *Rum*, and although the selling of it was expressly forbidden by the Provincial authorities, yet there was scarcely a treaty or conference without this potion being a part of the presents made by the *refined* white man to his *ignorant* red brother. Of a consequence liquor was sold, and we are told by Conrad Weiser that on one occasion "on the Sasquahannah," the Indians whom he was conducting to Philadelphia became so drunk that he was fearful of them and left them. At the period first referred to, it seems, a predatory band of Indians, on returning from the Carolinas, or the "Patowmack," naturally halted at John Harris'. In exchanging part of their goods, probably rum—for this seems to have been the principal beverage drunk at that period—was one of the articles in barter. At least we have it by tradition that the Indians became riotous in their drunken revelry; and demanding more rum, were refused by Mr. Harris, who began to fear harm from his visitors. Not to be denied, they again demanded liquor, and seizing him, they took him to a tree near by, binding him thereto. After helping themselves to whatever they wanted of his stores, they danced around the unhappy captive, who no doubt thought his death was nigh.

Prior to this, the Indian village of Paxtang had been deserted, and the inhabitants removed to the west side of the Susquehanna. On the bluff opposite John Harris', as also at the mouth of the Yellow Breeches, there were lodges of Shawanese, and these held our Indian trader in high esteem. Information was taken them by Mr. Harris' negro servant, when at once were summoned the warriors, who crossed the river, where, after a slight struggle with the drunken Indians, they rescued from a death of torture their white friend.

Although no mention of these facts is made in the Provincial records, there may possibly have been good reason therefor, and it is well known that many incidents, well authenticated in later years, have not been noted in the documents referred to. By tradition and private sources alone are they preserved from oblivion. It was no myth, this attempt to burn John Harris, and although the pen and pencil have joined in making therefrom a romance, and heightened it with many a gaudy coloring, yet accurate resources have furnished us with the details here given.

The remains of this tree, which in the memory of the oldest inhabitant bore fruit, stands within the enclosure at Harris park, a striking memento of that thrilling incident, and in this place and in this connection we propose to erect a substantial monument to the memory of that brave pioneer, that as the years roll on and that old stump crumbles into dust something may tell that story of frontier times. Let subscriptions of one dollar each be the limit, and 2,500 or 3,000 persons in a city of 30,-000 can readily be found with patriotism enough in their bosoms to contribute to this laudable design. Before the year closes I can assure my hearers, that the monument to the memory of those who fell in the war for the

Union will be completed. After that, the duty for which I speak will properly suggest itself.

Harris' trade with the Indians continued to increase, and Harris Ferry became known far and wide, not only to the red men, but to the white race in foreign countries.

During John Harris' frequent visits to Philadelphia he met at the house of his friend Shippen, Miss Esther Say, like himself not over young, from his native Yorkshire, and in the latter part of the year 1720 married her. The wedding took place either at the Swedes Church, Wicaco, or at Christ Church, both being members of the Church of England. Among the early colonists who settled in Philadelphia were a number of the name of Say, but to which family Esther Harris was connected is not to be ascertained with certainty. She was kinswoman to the Shippens, and of course respectably connected. A remarkable woman, she was also well calculated to share the love, the trials, the hardships and the cabin of the intrepid pioneer.

In 1721–22 their first child, Elizabeth, was born; in 1725 their second, Esther Harris, and in October, 1727, their first son, John Harris. This was the founder of Harrisburg. The statement that he was the first white male child born west of the Conewago Hills is not correct. There were settlers beyond, along the Swatara, as early as 1718; and it is natural to suppose that in many a log cabin the sunshine of boyhood gladdened the hearts of the hardy pioneer, and who also attained mature age. The parents carried their child when nearly a year old to Philadelphia, where he was baptized on the 22d of September, 1728, as they had previously done with their other children. That of Esther Harris took place August 31, 1726, according to the parish register of Christ Church, but we have not been able to ascertain the date of the baptism of the eldest child.

Until this period (1728) the country lying between the Conewago Hills and the Kittochtinny Mountains was owned, or rather claimed, by the Five Nations. It is true, the Scotch-Irish settlers had been pushed within these bounds ten years previously by the very Provincial authorities who destroyed their cabins on land already purchased. The treaty of 1728 opened up this vast and rich valley to the adventuresome. Filling up rapidly, on May 10, 1729, the Assembly passed "An act for the erecting the Upper Part of the Province of Pennsylvania lying towards the Sasquehannah, Conestogoe, Donnegal, etc., into a county," to be called Lancaster. At the first court in and for said county, November 3, 1730, at Posthlethwaite's, a petition was presented by John Harris, among others, "praying that he may be recommended to the Governor as a suitable person to trade with the Indians," and was allowed *per curiam*." This, of course, was necessary in the change of counties ; heretofore the application passed through the court of Chester county, and in this connection we may remark that among the Chester county records as early as 1722 is to be found the name of John Harris, "on the Sasquahannah." Subsequently he made application to the same authority to "sell rum by the small," which was granted.

In 1732, with the desire of establishing an additional trading-post, Harris built a store-house at the mouth of the Juniata. The last purchase (1728) not extending this far, the Indians objected to it, especially Sassonan and Shickalamy, who wrote through their interpreters to the Governor, informing him of the fact, and also to John

Harris, commanding him to desist from making a plantation at the point referred to. The authorities made no objection.

By virtue of a warrant from the Proprietaries of Pennsylvania, bearing date January 1, 1725–6, five hundred acres of land were granted to John Harris, father of the founder of Harrisburg; and subsequently, on the 17th of December, 1733, by a patent, three hundred acres of allowance land, upon which he had commenced a settlement, on the present site of the city, about the year 1717. The land included in the latter patent extended from what is now the line of Cumberland street some distance south of the present north boundary of the city, and including also a part of the present site of the city, with its several additions.

Until the year 1735–6, there was no regularly constructed road to the Susquehanna, but at a session of the Provincial Council held in Philadelphia January 22, 1735–6, on the petition of sundry inhabitants of Chester and Lancaster counties, "setting forth the Want of a High Road in the Remote parts of the said Counties where the petitioners are seated, and that a very commodious one may be laid out from the Ferry of John Harris, on Susquehannah, to fall in with the High Road leading from Lancaster town at or near the Plantation of Edward Kennison, in the Great Valley in the County of Chester," it was ordered that viewers be appointed who shall make a return of the same, "together with a Draught of the said Road." Subsequently this was done, and the highway opened from the Susquehanna to the Delaware, and in years after continued westward to the Ohio. As a matter of course, the laying out of this road increased greatly the business at Harris Ferry, and it became at a very early period the depot of trade to the western and northern frontiers of the Province, a position which it has held for over a century and a half.

Well advanced in life, at the age of about seventy-five, after having for several years intrusted his business to his eldest son, still in his minority, in December, 1748, the first pioneer quietly passed away from earth, having previously made a request that his remains be interred underneath the shade of that tree so memorable to him. There his dust lies at rest on the banks of our beautiful river—within the hearing of its thundering at flood-tide, and the musical rippling of its pellucid waters in its subdued majesty and beauty.

The oldest son, John Harris, who succeeded to the greatest portion of his father's estate, and who, in 1785, laid out the Capital City of Pennsylvania, married first Elizabeth M'Clure and second Mary Reed, daughter of Captain Adam Reed, of Hanover, an officer of the Provincial service, was a prominent personage during the Indian wars, and the principal military storekeeper on the frontier. His letters to the Governors of the Province and other officials are of intense interest, and deserve to be collated by our antiquarians. Not models of style, it is true, but they give vivid descriptions of the perilous times in which our ancestors dwelt who made the then out-bounds of civilization flourish and "blossom as a rose."

By a grant from Thomas Penn and Richard Penn, Esqs., proprietaries, to John Harris, Jr., bearing date of record "ye 19th February, 1753," that gentleman was allowed the right of running a ferry across the Susquehanna, from which originated the former name of the place, which previous to the organization of the county, was known far and near as Harris Ferry.

It appears from letters of John Harris, written to Governor Morris, that an Indian named Half-King, also called *Tanacharisson*, died at his house on the night of the 1st of October, 1754. Rupp says that "he had his residence at Logstown, on the Ohio, fourteen miles below Pittsburgh, on the opposite side. George Washington visited him in 1753, and desired him to relate some of the particulars of a journey he had shortly before made to the French Commandant at Fort Duquesne." We find this note among the votes of Assembly, 1754: "Dec. 17, Post Meridian, 1754.—The Committee of Accounts reported a balance of £10 15s. 4d. due to the said John Harris for his expenses, and £5 for his trouble, &c., in burying the Half-King and maintaining the sundry Indians that were with him."

They had considerable trouble at Harris Ferry during the French and Indian war, which extended over the period from 1754 to 1765. A petition from the inhabitants of the townships of Paxtang, Derry and Hanover, Lancaster county, bearing date July 22, 1754, and setting forth their precarious condition, was presented and read in the Council on the 6th of August following. It bore the signatures of Thomas Forster, James Armstrong, John Harris, Thomas Simpson, Samuel Simpson, John Carson, David Shields, William M'Mullin, John Cuoit, William Armstrong, William Bell, John Dougherty, James Atkin, Andrew Cochran, James Reed, Thomas Rutherford, T. M'Carter, William Steel, Samuel Hunter, Thos. Mayes, James Coler, Henry Rennicks, Richard M'Clure, Thomas Dugan, John Johnson, Peter Fleming, Thomas Sturgeon, Matthew Taylor, Jeremiah Sturgeon, Thos. King, Robert Smith, Adam Reed, John Crawford, Thomas Crawford, Jonathan M'Clure, Thomas Hume,

Thomas Steene, John Hume, John Creige, Thomas M'Clure, William M'Clure, John Rodgers, James Patterson, John Young, Ez. Sankey, John Forster, Mitchel Graham, James Toalen, James Galbraith, James Campbell, Robert Boyd, James Chambers, Robert Armstrong, Jno. Campbell, Hugh Black, Thomas Black.

At this period also we find an extensive correspondence between John Harris, Conrad Weiser and others and Edward Shippen, complaining of the insecurity of life and property owing to the depredations of the Indians; and their tenor is a continual and just complaint of the outrages committed by the savages, and urgent requests to the authorities for protection, and arms, etc.

On the 8th of January, 1756, a council with the Indians was held at the house of John Harris, at Paxtang, composed of Hon. Robert Hunter Morris, Governor; James Hamilton and Richard Peters, secretaries; Joseph Fox, commissioner, and Conrad Weiser, interpreter; two Indians of the Six Nations called "The Belt of Wampum," a Seneca, and the "Broken Thigh," a Mohawk. The meeting was of an amicable character, and was only the preliminary step to a larger and more important council held the week following at Carlisle. One of the reasons for holding the council at the latter place was, "that there were but few conveniences 'for the proper entertainment' of the Governor and his company at Harris Ferry, and Mr. Weiser gave it as his opinion that it would be better to adjourn to Carlise." A second council was held here on the 1st of April, 1757. Present: the Rev. John Elder, Captain Thomas M'Kee, Messrs. James Armstrong, Hugh Crawford, John Harris, William Pentrup, interpreter, and warriors from the Mohawks, Oneidas, Tuscaroras, Onondagoes, Nanticokes, Cayugas,

Delawares, Senecas and Conestogoes, with their women and children. George Croghan, Esq., deputy agent to the Hon. Sir W. Johnson, Bart., his majesty's sole agent and superintendent of the Six Nations, etc., was also present. This council was removed to Lancaster, owing to the number of Indians then encamped at Conestoga Manor, where the remainder of the business was concluded.

The most interesting event of this period was the extermination of the so-called Conestoga Indians by the Paxtang Rangers. The situation of the frontiers succeeding the Pontiax war was truly deplorable, principally owing to the supineness of the Provincial authorities, for the Quakers, who controlled the government, were, to use the language of Capt. Lazarus Stewart, "more solicitous for the welfare of the blood-thirsty Indian than for the lives of the frontiersmen. In their blind partiality, bigotry and political prejudice, they would not readily accede to the demands of those of a different religious faith. Especially was this the case relative to the Presbyterians and Roman Catholics, both of whom were tolerated by mere sufferance. To them, therefore, was greatly attributable the reign of horror and devastation in the border counties. The government was deaf to all entreaties, and General Amherst, commander of the British forces in America, did not hesitate to give his feelings an emphatic expression—*"The conduct of the Pennsylvania Assembly,"* he wrote, *"is altogether so infatuated and stupidly obstinate, that I want words to express my indignation thereat."* Nevertheless, the sturdy Scotch-Irish and Germans of this section rallied for their own defense. The inhabitants of Paxtang and Hanover immediately enrolled themselves into several companies, the Rev. John Elder being their Colonel.

Lazarus Stewart, Matthew Smith and Asher Clayton, men of acknowledged military ability and prowess, commanded distinct companies of Rangers. These brave men were ever on the alert, watching with eagle eye the Indian marauders who at this period swooped down upon the defenseless frontiers. High mountains, swollen rivers, or great distances never deterred or appalled them. Their courage and fortitude were equal to every undertaking, and woe betide the red men when their blood-stained tracks once met their eyes. The Paxtang Rangers were the terror of the Indians—they were swift on foot, excellent horsemen, good shots, skillful in pursuit or escape, dexterous as scouts and expert in manœuvering.

The murders in and around Paxtang, notwithstanding the vigilance of the Rangers, became numerous, and many a family mourned for some of their number shot by the secret foe or carried away captive. The frontiersmen took their rifles with them to the field and to the sanctuary. Their colonel and pastor placed his trusty piece beside him in the pulpit; and it is authoritatively stated that on one occasion old Derry meeting house was surrounded while he was preaching; but their spies having counted the rifles the Indians retired from their ambuscade without making an attack.

Many were the murderous deeds perpetrated by the savages—but where these came from was a mystery. Indians had been traced by the scouts to the wigwams of the so-called friendly Indians at Conestoga, and to those of the Moravian Indians in Northampton county. Suspicion was awakened, the questions, "are these Christian Indians treacherous? are their wigwams the harbors of our deadly foe? do they conceal the nightly prowling assassin of the forest : the villain, who with savage ferocity, tore the innocent babe from the bosom of its mother, where it had been quietly reposing, and hurled it in the fire? The mangled bodies of our friends cry aloud for vengeance." Such were the questions, surmises, and expressions of the exasperated people on the frontiers: and well warranted, for on one occasion when the Assembly were deaf to all entreaties and petition, with the hope of arousing their sympathy the murdered were taken to Philadelphia on wagons—when a prominent Quaker, with a sneer, remarked they were "only Irish." This unfeeling expression was remembered by the Scotch-Irish of the frontiers.

The Quakers who controlled the government, as heretofore remarked, "seemed resolved," says Parkman, "that they would neither defend the people of the frontier or allow them to defend themselves, vehemently inveighed against all expeditions to cut off the Indian marauders. Their security was owing to their local situation, being confined to the eastern part of the Province." That such was the case, rather than to the kind feelings of the Indian towards them, is shown by the fact that of the very few living in exposed positions, several were killed.

The inhabitants declared openly that they no longer confided in the professions of the Governor or his advisers in the Assembly. Numbers of volunteers joined the Rangers of Northampton, Berks, Lancaster, York and Cumberland, who were engaged in tracing the midnight assassins. On the Manor, a portion of land surveyed for the Proprietaries, situated in Lancaster county, near where the borough of Columbia is now located, was settled a band of squalid, miserable Indians—the refuse of sundry tribes. Time and again they were suspected of murder and thievery, and their movements at this crisis were closely watched. *Strange* Indians were constantly coming and going.

Colonel Elder under the date of September 13, 1763, thus wrote to Governor Hamilton, "I suggest to you the propriety of an immediate removal of the Indians from Conestoga and placing a garrison in their room. *In case this is done, I pledge myself for the future security of the frontiers.*"

Subsequently, on taking charge of the executive affairs of the Province in October, Governor John Penn replied as follows: "The Indians of Conestoga have been represented as innocent, helpless and dependent on this government for support. The faith of this government is pledged for their protection. I cannot remove them without adequate cause. The contract made with William Penn was a private agreement, afterwards confirmed by several treaties. Care has been taken by the provincial committee that no Indians but our own visit Conestoga. Whatever can be faithfully executed under the laws, shall be as faithfully performed;" and yet Governor Penn in writing to Thomas Penn afterwards uses this language: "Many of them," referring to the frontier inhabitants, "have had their wives and children murdered and scalped, their houses burnt to the ground, their cattle destroyed, and from an easy, plentiful life are now become beggars. In short, not only in this Province, but in the neighboring governments is the spirit of the people inveterate against the Indians."

John Harris had previously made a similar request: "The Indians here, I hope your honor will be pleased to be removed to some other place, *as I don't like their company.*"

The Rangers finding appeals to the authorities useless, resolved on taking the law into their own hands. Several Indian murderers had been traced to Conestoga, and it was determined to take them prisoners. Captain Stewart, whose men ascertained this fact, acquainted his colonel of the object, who seemed rather to encourage his command to make the trial, as an example was necessary to be made for the safety of the frontier inhabitants. The destruction of the Conestogas was not then projected. That was the result of the attempted capture. Parkman and Webster, following Rupp, state that Colonel Elder, learning of an intent to destroy the entire tribe, as they were about to set off rode after them commanding them to desist, and that Stewart threatened to shoot his horse. Such was not the case. From a letter dated Paxtang, December 16, 1763, written to Governor Penn, he says: "On receiving intelligence the 13th inst., that a number of persons were assembled on purpose to go and cut off the Conestoga Indians, in concert with Mr. Forster, the neighboring magistrate, I hurried off an express with *written message* to that party 'entreating them to desist from such an undertaking, representing to them the unlawfulness and barbarity of such an action; that it's cruel and unchristian in its nature, and would be fatal in its consequences to themselves and families; that private persons have no right to take the lives of any under the protection of the legislature; that they must, if they proceeded in that affair, lay their accounts to meet with a severe prosecution, and become liable even to capital punishment; that they need not expect that the country would endeavor to conceal or screen them from punishment, but that they would be detected and given up to the resentment of the government.' These things I urged in the warmest terms in order to prevail with them to drop the enterprise, but to no purpose."

Not to be deterred, the Rangers reached the Indian settlement before daylight. The barking of some dogs discovered them and a number of *strange Indians* rushed from their wigwams, brandishing their tomahawks. This show of resistance was sufficient inducement for the Rangers to make use of their arms. In a few moments every Indian present fell before the unerring fire of the brave frontiersmen. The act accomplished, they mounted their horses and returned severally to their homes. Unfortunately a number of the Indians were absent from Conestoga, prowling about the neighboring settlements, doubtless on predatory excursions. The destruction at the Manor becoming known, they were placed in the Lancaster work-house for protection. Among these vagabonds were two well known to Parson Elder's scouts.

An express being sent to Philadelphia with the news, great excitement ensued, and Governor Penn issued a proclamation relative thereto. Notwithstanding its fine array of words it fell upon the Province harmless. Outside of the Quaker settlements every one heartily approved of the measures taken by the Paxtang Rangers. As the Governor himself wrote to England: "If we had ten thousand of the King's troops I don't believe it would be possible to secure one of these people. Though I took all the pains I could even to get their names, I could not succeed, for indeed nobody would make the discovery, though ever so well acquainted with them, and there is not a magistrate in the country would have touched one of them. The people of this town are as inveterate against the Indians as the frontier inhabitants. For it is beyond a doubt that many of the Indians now in town [referring to the Moravian Indians confined in the barracks] have been concerned in committing murders among the back settlers."

The presence of the remaining Indians at Lancaster also became a cause of great uneasiness to the magistrates and people, for as previously remarked, two or three were notorious scoundrels. It may be here related that several of the *strange* Indians harbored at Conestoga, who were also absent at the destruction of the village, made their escape and reached Philadelphia, where they joined the Moravian Indians from Nain and Wechquetank, and there secreted.

The removal of the remaining Indians from Lancaster was requested by the chief magistrate, Edward Shippen. Governor Penn proved very tardy, and we are of the opinion he cared little about them, or he would have acted promptly, as from his own confession he was not ignorant of the exasperation of the people and the murderous character of the refugees. Day after day passed by, and the excitement throughout the frontiers became greater. The Rangers, who found that their work had been only half done, consulted as to what measure should be further proceeded with. Captain Stewart proposed to capture the principal Indian outlaw, who was confined in the Lancaster work-house, and take him to Carlisle jail, where he could be held for trial. This was heartily approved, and accordingly a detachment of the Rangers, variously estimated at from twenty to fifty, proceeded to Lancaster on the 27th of December, broke into the work-house, and but for the show of resistance would

8

have effected their purpose. But the younger portion of the Rangers, to whom was confided this work, were so enraged at the defiance of the Indians, that before their resentment could be repressed by Captain Stewart, the unerring rifle was employed, and the last of the so-called Conestogas had yielded up his life. In a few minutes thereafter, mounting their horses, the daring Rangers were safe from arrest. George Gibson, who, from his acquaintance with the principal frontiersmen of his time, in a letter written some years after, gives the most plausible account of this transaction, which bore such an important part in the early history of the Province. He says: "No murder has been committed since the removal of the friendly Indians and the destruction of the Conestogas—a strong proof that the murders were committed under the cloak of the Moravian Indians. A description of an Indian who had, with great barbarity, murdered a family on the Susquehanna, near Paxtang, was sent to Lazarus Stewart at Lancaster. This Indian had been traced to Conestoga. On the day of its destruction he was on a hunting expedition. When he heard that the Rangers were in pursuit of him he fled to Philadelphia. The three or four who entered the workhouse, at Lancaster, were directed by Stewart to seize on the murderer, and give him to his charge. When those outside heard the report of the guns within, several of the Rangers alighted, thinking their friends in danger, and hastened to the door. The more active of the Indians, endeavoring to make their escape, were met by them and shot. No children were killed by the Paxtang boys. No act of savage butchery was committed."

If the excitement throughout the Province was great after the affair at Conestoga, this last transaction set everything in a ferment, "No language," says Rev. Dr. Wallace, "can describe the outcry which arose from the Quakers in Philadelphia, or the excitement which swayed to and fro in the frontiers and in the city." The Quakers blamed the Governor, the Governor the Assembly, and the latter censured everybody except their own inaction. Two proclamations were issued by the Provincial authorities, offering rewards for the seizure of those concerned in the destruction of the Indians; but this was impossible, owing to the exasperation of the frontiersmen, who heartily approved of the action of the Rangers.

On the 27th of December the Rev. Mr. Elder hurriedly wrote to Governor Penn: "The storm, which had been so long gathering, has at length exploded. Had government removed the Indians from Conestoga, as was frequently urged without success, this painful catastrophe might have been avoided. What could I do with men heated to madness? All that I could do was done. I expostulated, but life and reason were set at defiance, and yet the men, in private life are virtuous and respectable— not cruel, but mild and merciful. * * * *The time will arrive when each palliating circumstance will be calmly weighed. This deed, magnified into the blackest of crimes, shall be considered one of those youthful ebullitions of wrath caused by momentary excitement, to which human infirmity is subjected.*"

To this extenuating and warm-hearted letter came a reply, under date of December 29, 1763, from the Governor, requesting the commanders of the troops—Colonels Elder and Seely—to return the provincial arms, etc., as their services were no longer required. From this letter of Governor John Penn, it is evident that the commissioners, or rather the Provincial council, intended

to punish both Colonel Elder and Esquire Seely, or that
with the destruction of the Conestogas, there was little or
no danger of Indian atrocities. The latter proved to be
the case, but the authorities were cognizant of the fact
that the Paxtang boys were correct in their surmisings,
and that peace would follow the removal of the friendly
Indians. It shows, also, that believing thus, the Provincial authorities were culpable to a great degree, in allowing the Indians to remain on the Manor, despite the rep-
resentations of Colonel Elder, John Harris and Edward
Shippen. The Reverend Mr. Elder quietly laid by his
sword, feeling confident that time would vindicate his
course, whatever that may have been.

Of the marching of the Paxtang boys towards Philadelphia, we shall briefly refer in this connection, and the reason therefor is best given by an extract from a letter of
Governor Penn: "The 14th of this month we suspect a
Thousand of the Rioters in Town to insist upon the Assembly granting their request with regard to the increase
of Representatives, to put them upon an equality with the
rest of the Counties. They have from time to time presented several petitions for the purpose, which have been
always disregarded by the House; for which reason they
intend to come in Person." Although our Quaker his-
torians have uniformly stated that the object of the Paxtang Boys was the massacre of the Moravian Indians in
Philadelphia, yet the foregoing statement of the Executive of the Province proves conclusively that their visit
was not one of slaughter but of petition for redress of
grievances. The narrative is one of interest to us in this
section and the true history remains to be written.

Pamphlets, says Webster, without number, truth or
decency, poured like a torrent from the press. The

Quakers took the pen to hold up the deed to execration; and many others seized the opportunity to defame' the Irish Presbyterians as ignorant bigots and lawless marauders.

Violent and bitter as were the attacks of the Quaker pamphleteers, Parson Elder was only casually alluded to. With the exception of the following, written to Col. Burd, he made no attempt to reply to any of these, leaving his cause with God and posterity: "Lazarus Stewart is still threatened by the Philadelphia party; he and his friends talk of leaving; if they do, the Province will lose some of its best friends, and that by the faults of others, not their own; for if any cruelty was practiced on the Indians, at Conestoga or at Lancaster, it was not by his or their hands.   There is great reason to believe that much injustice has been done to all concerned.   In the contrariness of accounts, we must infer that much rests for support on the imagination or interest of the witnesses. The character of Stewart and his friends were well established.   Ruffians, nor brutal, they were not; but humane, liberal and moral, nay, religious.   It is evidently not the wish of the party to give Stewart a fair hearing. All he desires is to be put on trial at Lancaster, near the scenes of the horrible butcheries committed by the Indians at Tulpenhocken, etc., where he can have the testimony of the scouts and rangers, men whose services can never be sufficiently rewarded.   The pamphlet has been sent by my friends and enemies; it failed to inflict a wound; it is at least a garbled statement; it carries with it the seeds of its own dissolution.   That the hatchet was used is denied, and is it not reasonable to suppose that men, accustomed to the use of guns, would make use of their favorite weapons?

"The inference is plain, that the *bodies* of the Indians were thus *mangled* after death by certain persons, to excite a feeling against the Paxtang boys. This fact Stewart says he can and will establish in a fair trial at Lancaster, York or Carlisle. At any rate we are all suffering at present by the secret influence of a faction—a faction who have shown their love to the Indians by not exposing themselves to its influence in the frontier settlements."

The "pamphlet" alluded to in the foregoing was the notorious article written by Benjamin Franklin for political effect. He acknowledged, in a letter to Lord Kames, that his object was a political one. As such, its tissue of falsehoods caused his defeat for member of the Assembly, a position he had held for fourteen years. Fortunately for him, the Revolution brought him into prominence, and the past was forgotten.

This transaction was subsequently "investigated" by the magistrate at Lancaster, but so condemnatory of the Indians was the evidence elicited that *it was the Quaker policy to suppress and destroy it*. Nevertheless all efforts to carry into effect the proclamation of the Governor was really suspended, so far as his authority went, in regard to which grave complaints were made by the Assembly, who seemed to bend all their energies to persecute the offenders.

The names of many of those brave defenders of their homes have been lost to us—but the frequent statement in all our histories that the participants in that transaction came to an untimely end, is false. With the exception of Lazarus Stewart, who fell on that unfortunate day at the massacre of Wyoming, these heroes of the frontiers lived to hearty old age, and several reached almost the hundred years of life. Their deeds were those of desperation, it is true, but their acts are to be honored and their names revered.

The discussions which ensued may truly be said to have sown the seeds of the Revolution, and in a letter of Governor John Penn to his brother in England, written at this time, he thus alludes to the inhabitants of Paxtang, "their next move will be to subvert the government and establish one of their own."

No wonder then, when the first mutterings of the storm was heard, that the people of this entire section were ripe for revolution. The love of liberty was a leading trait of the people who settled this delightful valley. The tyranny and oppression of Europe drove them to seek an asylum among the primeval forests of America. Persecution for conscience' sake compelled alike the Scotch-Irish and the German of the Palatinate to come hither and rear their altars dedicated to God and Freedom to man. With them Independence was as much their dream as the realization. Their isolated position—placed on the frontiers—unprotected by the Provincial authorities—early instilled into their minds those incentives to action, that when the opportune moment arrived they were in the van. Two years before the Declaration by Congress, the people had assembled at their respective places of rendezvous, and heralded forth their opinions in plain and unmistakable language, while the citizens of the large towns were fearful and hesitating.

As early as the spring of 1774 meetings were held in the different townships, the resolves of only two of which are preserved to us. The earliest was that of an assembly of the inhabitants of Hanover, Lancaster county, held on Saturday, June 4, 1774. Colonel Timothy Green, chairman, "to express their sentiments on the present critical state of affairs." It was then and there "Unanimously resolved:"

"1st. That the recent action of the Parliament of Great Britain is iniquitous and oppressive.

"2d. That it is the bounden duty of the inhabitants of America to oppose every measure which tends to deprive them of their just prerogatives.

"3d. That in a closer union of the colonies lies the safeguard of the people.

"4th. That in the event of Great Britain attempting to force unjust laws upon us by the strength of arms, our cause we leave to Heaven and our rifles.

"5th. That a committee of nine be appointed who shall act for us and in our behalf as emergency may require.

"The committee consisted of Col. Timothy Green, Jas. Caruthers, Josiah Espy, Robert Dixon, Thomas Copenheffer, William Clark, James Stewart, Joseph Barnett and John Rogers."

So much for patriotic Hanover. Following in the footsteps of these brave men, on Friday following, June 10, 1774, a similar meeting was held at Middletown, Col. James Burd, chairman, at which these stirring resolves were concurred in, and which served as the text of those passed at the meeting at Lancaster subsequently:

"1st. That the acts of the Parliament of Great Britain in divesting us of the right to give and grant our money, and assuming such power to themselves, are unconstitutional, unjust and oppressive.

"2d. That it is an indispensable duty we owe to ourselves and posterity to oppose with decency and firmness every measure tending to deprive us of our just rights and privileges.

"3d. That a close union of the Colonies and their faithful adhering to such measures as a general Congress shall judge proper, are the most likely means to procure redress of American grievances and settle the rights of the Colonies on a permanent basis.

"4th. That we will sincerely and heartily agree to and abide by the measures which shall be adopted by the members of the general Congress of the Colonies.

"5th. That a committee be appointed to confer with similar committees relative to the present exigency of affairs."

Not to be behind their Scotch-Irish neighbors, the German inhabitants located in the east of the county, met at Frederickstown, (now Hummelstown,) on Saturday, the 11th of June, at which Captain Frederick Hummel was chairman, resolving to stand by the other townships in all their action.

We say they were ripe for revolution, and when the stirring battle-drum aroused the new-born nation, the inhabitants of Dauphin valiantly armed for the strife. One of the first companies raised in the Colonies was that of Captain Matthew Smith, of Paxtang. Within ten days after the receipt of the news of the battle of Lexington, this company was armed and equipped, ready for service. Composing this pioneer body of patriots was the best blood of the county—the Dixons, the Elders, the Simpsons, the Boyds, the Harrises, the Reeds, the Tods and others. Archibald Steele and Michael Simpson were the lieutenants. It was the second company to arrive at Boston, coming south of the Hudson river. It was subsequently ordered to join General Arnold in his unfortunate campaign against Quebec, and the most reliable account of that expedition was written by a member of this very

Paxtang company, John Joseph Henry, afterwards President Judge of Lancaster and Dauphin counties. They were enlisted for one year. The majority, however, were taken prisoners at Quebec, while a large per centage died of wounds and exposure.

In March, 1776, Capt. John Murray's company was raised in Paxtang township, attached to the rifle battalion of Col. Samuel Miles. The officers of this company were First Lieutenant, John Stoner, May 15, 1776; Second Lieutenant, James Hamilton, March 16, 1776; and Third Lieutenant, Charles Taylor, March 19, 1776. The last named was killed at the battle of Long Island, August 27, 1776. This company participated in the bat tles of Long Island, White Plains, Princeton and Trenton.

Captain Patrick Anderson's company was raised in the lower part of the county in January, 1776. It was attached to Col. Atlee's musketry battalion, suffered severely at Long Island, re-organized under Captain Ambrose Crain, a gallant officer, placed in the Pennsylvania State regiment of foot, commanded by Col. John Bull, and subsequently, in the re-arrangement of the line, the 13th Pennsylvania, under Col. Walter Stewart, so conspicuous in the battle of Yorktown.

Captain John Marshal's company was from Hanover, enlisted in March, 1776, and attached to Col. Miles' battalion, participating in the various battles in which that brave command distinguished itself. Of this company the remaining officers were First Lieutenant, John Clark, March 15, 1776; Second Lieutenant, Thomas Gourley, March 15, 1776, promoted to First Lieutenant of the 9th Pennsylvania, December 7, 1776; Third Lieutenant, Stephen Hanna, March 19, 1776.

Captain Smith's company, on the expiration of their term of service, re-enlisted in the First Pennsylvania

(Col. Hand,) with Captain Michael Simpson, December, 1776, who retired from the army January 1, 1781. David Harris commanded a company in this regiment July 1776 (resigned October, 1777,) of which also James Hamilton, formerly lieutenant in Capt. John Murray's company, was promoted major (retiring January 1, 1783.) Major Hamilton was captured at the battle of Brandywine.

In the Tenth Pennsylvania (Colonel Joseph Penrose) were Captain John Stoner's company, December 4, 1776; and Capt. Robert Sample's, December 4, 1776, (retired January 1, 1781.) John Steel, First Lieutenant of the former company, was killed at Brandywine September 11, 1777.

In the Twelfth Pennsylvania (Col. William Cook) was the company of Capt. John Harris, October 14, 1776; First Lieutenant, John Reily, October 16, 1776 (subsequently promoted to Captain, and mustered out with the regiment November 3, 1783;) Second Lieutenant, John Carothers, October 16, 1776, (killed at Germantown.)

The foregoing were the different companies raised in this part of the country at the *outset* of the Revolution— ere the thunder-tones of the Declaration of Independence sounded along the corridors of time. Following those in succession were the Associators, the brave minute-men,

> "Who left the ploughshare in the mould,
> Their flocks and herds without a fold,
> The sickle in the unshorn grain,
> The corn, half garner'd on the plain,
> And muster'd, in their simple dress,
> For wrongs to seek a stern redress,
> To right those wrongs, come weal, come woe,
> To perish, or o'ercome the foe."

At one period the entire country was so bare of men that the old men, the women and the lads of ten and twelve years not only done the planting and harvesting, but took up arms to defend their homes in the threatened invasion by Indians and tories after the massacre of Wyoming.

At Trenton, at Princeton, at Brandywine and Germantown, at the Crooked Billet and the Paoli, the militia of Dauphin fought, and bled, and died. With over one hundred and fifty commissioned officers, of whom my friend, Mr. Hamilton, has so well referred to, there certainly must have been a powerful force. After what has been said, I need scarcely refer to the gallant Burd, Crouch, Green, Weir, Cox, Boyd, Graham, Forrest, Allen and Lee; or the chivalric Stewart, Murray, Wilson, Wiggins and Rogers—and that long line of heroes whose brilliant achievements shed an undying glory on the patriotism of Dauphin county in the Revolution. What was once said of the men of New England can more truthfully be said of our own county, and of Pennsylvania especially:

"* * * On every hill they lie,
　　On every field of strife made red
　By bloody victory.
　　Each valley, where the battle pour'd
　　Its red and awful tide,
　　Beheld "Old Dauphin's bravest" sword
　With slaughter deeply dyed.
　　Their bones are on the Northern hill
　And on the Southern plain,
　　By brook and river, lake and rill,
　And by the roaring main.

"The land is holy where they fought,
　　And holy where they fell,
　For by their blood that land was bought,
　　The land they loved so well.
　Then glory to that valiant band,
　The honor'd saviours of the land!"

When liberty shall have been crushed to earth—then, and then only will their deeds and their sweet memories be effaced from the hearts of their descendants.

With the dawn of peace, the people of the county returned to their usual avocations. Civil affairs were taken cognizance of, and movements were at once made to secure the formation of a new county, with Harrisburg as the seat of justice. By the act of Assembly of March 4, 1785, the county of Dauphin was separated from Lancaster, its name derived from the eldest son of the then king of the French—France at that period, in consequence of its efficient aid to the Colonies, being uppermost in the affections of the people. The enthusiasm was unbounded, and, as we shall refer to hereafter, carried to extreme lengths. The name was suggested by the prime movers for the formation of the new county. The seat of justice was fixed at Harris' Ferry, then a village of about one hundred houses, although the town was not actually laid out or surveyed until-after the passage of the ordinance referred to. In the commissions of the officers of the new county, the town was named Louisburgh, in honor of Louis XVI., suggested by Chief Justice Thomas M'Kean, not only on account of his French leanings, but to show his petty spite against Mr. Harris, to whom, somehow or other, he held political opposition.

This act of injustice was subsequently remedied, when, on the 13th of April, 1791, the town was created a borough, by the name of Harrisburg. It was undecided for awhile whether to call the place Harris' *Ferry* or Harris-*burg*. The latter, fortunately, was adopted.

On the organization of the county, Middletown was the largest village in the county, and strenuous efforts were made by its citizens and the inhabitants of the townships subsequently forming Lebanon county, to make it the seat of justice; while similar claims were made for the town of Lebanon, on account of its central location.

The machinery of the new county was soon put into motion, the earliest record of whose courts reads thus:

"At a court of quarter sessions, holden near Harris' Ferry, in and for the county of Dauphin," &c., on the "third Tuesday of May, in the year of our Lord 1785," before "Timothy Green, Samuel Jones and Jonathan M'-Clure, Esqrs., justices of the same court."

We may imagine the scene, in a small room in a log house near the "lower ferry," at Front and Vine streets, with a jury particularly intelligent—an excellent set of county officers, and such a bar as Ross, Kittera, Chambers, Hubley, James Biddle, Hanna, Andrew Dunlop, Reily, Collinson Reed, Jasper Yeates, John Joseph Henry, Thomas Duncan, and Thomas Smith, most of whom rose to occupy the highest positions at the bar or in the Senate—quite a show of famous men to start the judicial engine of the new county, with the net result of convicting William Courtenay, a descendant of one of the proudest houses of England, and sentencing him to eighteen lashes, fifteen shillings fine, and "to stand in the pillory." This instrument of judicial vengeance stood about sixty yards below the grave of John Harris, the elder, or just above the ferry house, at the junction of Front and Paxtang streets. This, doubtless, was the exact position, as two or three of the first courts were held in a building on what is now the southern corner of Front street and Washington avenue. There was no citizen of Harrisburg on the first jury, except, perhaps, Alexander Berryhill, but that is not certain. Colonel James Cowden, of Lower Paxtang township, was the foreman of this grand jury.

The sheriff of Lancaster county exercised the same office in Dauphin county. The names of the jurymen were James Cowden, (foreman,) Robert Montgomery, John Gilchrist, Barefoot Brunson, John Clarke, Roan M'Clure, John Carson, John Wilson, Wm. Crane, Archibald M'Allister, Richard Dixon, John Pattimore, James Crouch, Jacob Awl, William Brown, Andrew Stewart, James Rogers, Samuel Stewart, John Cooper, Alexander Berryhill. Alexander Graydon was the first prothonotary, and Anthony Kelker the first sheriff.

The minutes of the second court held in the town are dated at "Harrisburgh," and on the 3d of August, 1786, the following endorsement appears on the docket: The name of the county town, or seat of the courts, is altered from "Harrisburgh" to "Louisburgh," in consequence of the Supreme Executive Council of the Commonwealth, so styling it in the Commissions of the Justices of said town."

The courts were held for several successive years in the same locality, but subsequently in the log house recently demolished on the south-east corner of Market street and Dewberry alley. From here it was removed to its present location, except during the sessions of the Legislature from 1812 to 1822, when the court occupied the brick building built by the county commissioners on the corner of Walnut street and Raspberry alley. The present edifice was erected in 1860.

The act of Assembly erecting Harrisburg into a borough defined its limits as follows:

"Beginning at low-water mark on the eastern shore of the Susquehanna River; thence by the pine-apple tree north 60¼ degrees, east 79 perches, to an ash tree on the west bank of Paxton Creek; thence by the several corners thereof 323 perches, to a white hickory on William Maclay's line; thence by the same south 67¾ degrees, west 212 perches, to a marked chestnut-oak on the eastern bank of the Susquehanna; thence by the same course to low-water mark to the place of beginning."

The borough limits were extended by the act of the 16th of April, 1838, as follows: "The north-western boundary line of the borough of Harrisburg shall be and the same is hereby extended and enlarged as follows: Extending it along the river line to the upper line of the land of the late William Maclay, on said river; thence to Paxton creek, and thence along said creek to the north-western corner to the present boundary." Thus annexing Maclaysburg, or all the territory included in the borough then lying north-west of South street.

During the so-called Whisky Insurrection, 1794, Harrisburg became quite prominent, it being on the great thoroughfare to the Western counties. The court house was then building, and some of the sympathizers with the anti-excise men beyond the mountains hoisted a French flag on that structure. Of course this gave offense and it was quietly removed. Several arrests were made of individuals who expressed sympathy for the Western insurgents—one of whom, Major Swiney, was confined in prison for nearly a year, when he was released without trial. Governor Mifflin, who was an excellent stump-speaker, made one of his characteristic addresses here, and in two days time no less than three companies from the town were on their march to Carlisle. When Gov. Howell, of New Jersey, and his brilliant staff remained over night, they were so hospitably entertained by the citizens that he returned his thanks in special orders.

On Friday, the 3d of October, when the President, the great and good Washington, approached the town, he was met by a large concourse of the people and the enthusiasm was unbounded. The worthy burgesses, Conrad Bombaugh and Alexander Berryhill, presented the address of the town, to which the chief magistrate briefly replied, bearing "testimony to the zealous and efficient exertions" they had made. That evening he held a reception at his head-quarters, where the principal citizens embraced the opportunity of paying their respects to the venerated chieftain. On the morning of the 4th he crossed the river at the upper ferry, which was fifty yards above the present Harrisburg bridge.

About this period came the fever of 1793–5 and the mill-dam troubles. For two years previous a disease of a malignant type prevailed during the summer season in the borough. Its origin was proved beyond doubt to be due to a mill-dam located in what is now the First ward of the city, on Paxtang creek. In 1793, during the prevalence of the yellow fever in Philadelphia, it was thought and even pronounced such. Quite a number of Irish emigrants died, and although many of the inhabitants were attacked there were no fatal cases among them. This was proof positive that the endemic was due to the damming up of the Paxtang creek, which was always "dead water," (its Indian significance,) producing malarial poisoning. Our ancestors, reasoning rightly, their next move was to get rid of the nuisance. Meetings were held, committees appointed, funds raised and tendered to the owners of the mill, Peter and Abraham Landis, the amount demanded by them the previous year for their property. The impecunious millers now required a greater sum, but the citizens positively refused, and at

10

a public meeting they resolved that a further tender be made the Landises and in case of refusal to "prostrate the dam" and pay, if necessary, the "proportionable parts of all legal expenses and damages that might accrue on any suits or indictments which might be brought or prosecuted in consequence of such acts." Our forefathers were not to be trifled with, and suiting the action to the word, met at a given hour and opened the dam. Eventually the parties compromised—the Landises accepted a certain sum and the town secured the mill right. The valuable papers relating to this interesting epoch in the history of Harrisburg are in the possession of the Dauphin County Historical Society and being prepared for publication. The entire transaction was creditable to the ancient Harrisburger, and the descendants of the men who then stood up for the rights of the people are among the most prominent of our citizens to-day.

In 1798, when a war with France was imminent and a call made by the general government on Pennsylvania for troops, an unusual excitement was created, and several companies tendered their services to the Governor. The storm blew over, and as in 1807, when a war was threatened with Great Britain—no occasion for troops were required, until five years after—when the second struggle with England took place. Among the prominent military organizations which armed for the conflict were the companies of Captains Thomas Walker, Richard M. Crain, John Carothers, Jeremiah Rees, Thomas M'Ilhenny, Peter Snyder, John B. Moorhead, James Todd, Richard Knight, John Elder, Isaac Smith, Philip Fedderhoff and Gawen Henry, quite a formidable array. Some of these marched as far as Baltimore at the time of the British attack on that city, while others went no farther than York. None of these companies had an opportunity to meet the enemy on the sanguinary field—but Dauphin county men composed the major portion of two companies which joined the Canada expedition. The heroes of this conflict are nearly all passed from off the stage of life. Following in the footsteps of the fathers of the Revolution, they emulated their heroism and devotion to the liberties of their country.

In the war with Mexico, consequent upon the annexation of Texas, among the troops which went out to that far-off land to vindicate the honor of our country and preserve its prestige, was the Cameron Guards, under command of Captain Edward C. Williams. They made a good record, their heroic conduct at Cerro Gordo, Chapultepec and the Garreta de Belina, won for them high renown and the commendation of their venerated commander-in-chief. Scarce a corporal's guard remains of that gallant band.

Coming down to later times, when the perpetuity of the Union was threatened, and the great North rose up like a giant in its strength to crush secession and rebellion, the events are so fresh in the remembrances of all that we shall only refer to them in brief. The first public meeting held after the firing upon Fort Sumter in the State of Pennsylvania, and in fact the first in any northern city, was in the court house at Harrisburg, General Simon Cameron being chairman thereof. Dauphin county, foremost in tendering men and means to the government for that bitter, deadly strife, furnished her full quota of volunteers. Twice Harrisburg was the objective point of the Confederate troops, and at one time (June, 1863) the enemy's picket was within two miles of the city. Active preparations were made for its defense, and fortifications erected on the bluff opposite, and named "Fort Washington." This was the only fortification deserving a name erected in any of the Northern States. Rifle pits were dug along the banks of the river, in front of Harris Park, and every preparation made to give the enemy a warm reception. The Union victory at Gettysburg checked the further advance of the Confederates, and with it the last attempt to invade the North. It would take volumes to rehearse not only the heroism of the sons of Dauphin county on the battle-field, but the deeds of mercy and charity and love of the noble-hearted women. Need we speak of the gallantry of the lamented Simmons and the six hundred brave dead—stricken down on the field of battle, in the hospital or in the loathsome prison, or yet of the living—Knipe and Jennings, the Awls, Porter, Williams and Jordan, Witman and Davis, Detweiler, M'Cormick and Alleman, Savage and Hummel, and many others—a long line of illustrious names—officers and privates of that immense force which Dauphin county sent out from her midst for the preservation of the Union.

The location of the first and greatest military camp in the Northern States was within the limits of Harrisburg—named, by Generals Knipe and Williams in honor of the Chief Magistrate of Pennsylvania, Camp Curtin, which with being the central point of communication, especially with the oft-beleagured Federal Capital, made it a prominent rendezvous. Our citizens were equal to any emergency, and a community which fed gratuitously 20,000 returned soldiers, repel with disdain the insinuation made by a malicious correspondent of a New York newspaper, that our people charged soldiers ten cents for a glass of water. This statement is equally reliable with that at the outset of the war, when the same newspapers ignorantly displayed at the head of their columns "Harrisburg protected by the Federal gunboats."

From the commencement of the war, the charity of the citizens was unbounded and without stint, the doors of hospitality freely opened, and to our honor be it said, two citizens, Messrs. John B. Simon and Eby Byers, established the Soldiers' Rest, where the sick and wounded patriot, on his way homeward, found rest, and refreshment, and gentle care. Thousands were kindly ministered to, and until the "boys came marching home" the good work went on unabated. In every cemetery and graveyard within the borders of Dauphin county lie the remains of her brave and true sons, while in the cemetery at Harrisburg the grass grows green over the graves of Union and Confederate soldiers from far-off States. In all the struggles for life, for liberty, for right and for the Union, Dauphin county has been in the van. But these dark days of our country have passed like "a dream that has been told." May the lesson taught be heeded by those who come after us—that the Union of States is not a rope of sand which may be broken at the will of any section.

The first newspaper enterprise in the county was by Major Eli Lewis, but even its name and date of issue are lost. The first permanent effort, however, in that line of which copies are extant, was *The Oracle of Dauphin, and Harrisburg Advertiser*, the initial number bearing date October 20, 1792, John Wyeth, editor and proprietor. Its forerunner was probably *The Harrisburg Advertiser*. The history of newspaperdom at Harrisburg is eventful as it is interesting. When the town became the capital of the State, which it did in 1812, unnumbered ventures were made in that line. Nearly all tell the same story—premature decay. In 1830, with a population of a little over 4,000 inhabitants, Harrisburg contained twelve printing offices, six book binderies, publishing eleven newspapers and one periodical, with an invested capital of over seventy-three thousand dollars. Of course that was not the era of railroads and telegraphs, and newspapers could spring up, and live a while and be extinguished without serious loss. The entire circulation of all these papers was not equal to either one of the daily issues of the *Telegraph* or *Patriot*.

The subject of internal improvements was one which early commanded the attention of the citizens of Pennsylvania, and one hundred years ago, as now, communication with the western country was the great aim of the business men of Philadelphia. The first effort was the removal of obstructions in the various streams, and especially that of the Susquehanna river; and although a considerable amount of money was eventually spent in improving the navigation thereof, the result was far from satisfactory. Previous to the Revolution, (1774,) the attention of the Provincial Assembly was called to this matter, and as a preliminary, it was proposed to lay out a town or city on that stream. John Harris, the founder of our city, immediately gave notice of his intention of laying out a town, which seemed to quiet the movement of undoubted land speculators. The Revolution coming on, such enterprises, if ever seriously considered, were abandoned. No sooner, however, came peace, than the business activity of the people sought out new channels—roads were made, attempts at slackwater navigation ventured on—until finally the Pennsylvania canal, from Columbia to Pittsburgh, opened up an avenue to trade, and brought prosperity to all the towns on its route. On none had it better effect than Middletown and Harrisburg, and the former place at one period was destined to retain a supremacy in population, enterprise, wealth and influence. It was a great lumber mart; the Union canal, and its admirable location, always made it a rival to the Capital City.

Previous to the opening of the Pennsylvania canal, the transportation facilities of the town were confined to Troy coaches or stages for passengers, and Conestoga wagons, great lumbering vehicles with semi-circular tops of sail-cloth, drawn by six stalwart horses, for goods of various descriptions. This was expensive—and the completion of the public improvements was an eventful era in the progress and development of this locality. Real estate advanced, commission and other merchants established themselves on the line of the canal, rope and boat manufactories were erected and various enterprises inaugurated, giving new life to the town and thrift and prosperity to the people. Several lines of passenger packets were established, and it was considered a wonderful thing when four packet boats arrived and departed in a single day. The consuming of three days and a half to go to Pittsburgh began to be deemed slow, and the building of railroads opened up another era in the development of the country. In September, 1836, the first train of cars entered the limits of Harrisburg over the Harrisburg, Portsmouth, Mount Joy and Lancaster railroad. Following this effort, other rapid transit enterprises were carried forward to completion until at the present time—when no less than one hundred trains of passenger cars arrive and leave Harrisburg daily for different points. We give these facts to show not only how great the travel, but the wonderful progress made in transit.

Previous to the year 1841, the pump or well was the only source of water supply, for drinking purposes, and the rain-barrel or cistern for other uses. When this is contrasted with the present abundance of that fluid, and the old fire engines of that day with the ponderous steam apparatus of the present, we wonder how the goodly citizens of forty years ago managed to get along. They were not as wasteful as we are; the river was nigh, it is true, but water carriage cost considerable in large families when required for laundry purposes. The most serious difficulty was in cases of fire, and frequently the pumps giving out the lines were formed to the river, of men, women and children, and the supply secured from thence. In those days every one went to the fire; there was work for all, old and young—the leathern buckets were required to be on hand, and all business was suspended while a conflagration was in progress. Far different now. The alarm sounds, and we listen to count the stroke—find out the location—and, should it be at a distance, we quietly resume our duties, knowing our presence is not required, for the brave and disinterested firemen with their engines are there and no fears are awakened as to the result. This feeling of security actuates us all, and yet how seldom do we think to whom we are so deeply indebted. It is the brave fireman who is fighting the mad flames, who is endangering his life for our property, and the safety, perchance of our little ones. To him is due the highest meed of praise—surpassing the valor of him who treads the wine-press of the battle-field. All honor to the ever-ready, intrepid fireman !

The first fire engine purchased by the citizens of Harrisburg was the "Union." Contemporaneous with this primitive machine were the Hope and Friendship, both of which organizations are in the highest state of efficiency to-day. When their Centennial comes around may "we all be there to see." The Citizen, the Washington, the Mount Vernon, the Paxton, the Good Will and the Lochiel were organized from 1836 to 1874, in the order named. We have alluded to their valuable services. A grateful community will ever stand by them.

On the 18th day of September, 1841, the water works were completed at a total expense of $120,000—a large sum in those days, but meagre compared with the sum expended in erecting the present extensive ones—which reach well on to a million of dollars. To no one is this community more deeply indebted for the successful carrying out the plan of the original water works than to Gen. William Ayres, a distinguished lawyer and citizen of Harrisburg, and for many years the president of the town council. To his energy, forethought and enterprise, these with other municipal improvements were brought to successful completion—and his name and services deserve kindly remembrance on this occasion.

To notice the various events which have transpired in the county and town is the duty of the faithful annalist— but time, if naught else, forbids. A summary, however, of such as may be of especial interest we recall for preservation.

The statistics of the churches have been given by Rev. Dr. Robinson. After these organizations the oldest association in the county, ante-dating the laying out of the town of Harrisburg, is Perseverance Lodge, No. 21, of Free and Accepted Masons, constituted in November, 1779, and styled among the records as the "Lodge at Paxtang." Its first members were officers of the Revolution, and through its existence of nearly a hundred years it has enrolled the names of many distinguished in the annals of the county and State—heroes, statesmen and divines, with men of all professions and trades—while *its* charity which has never been a "sounding brass and tinkling cymbal" has been without stint.

Of library companies various attempts were made from the year 1791 for a period of fifty years, to establish them—all proving unsuccessful. That there is no large public library and reading room in our city is far from creditable to the intelligence or liberality of our citizens, and it is hoped that measures will be taken for such an enterprise. It is only by endowment that such will prove permanent, and until this can be accomplished propositions are useless and of little avail. Society private libraries are not permanent. These have their uses—but a free public library will alone meet the wants of a rapidly-growing and a reading community like ours. Too much dependence has been placed in the library of the State—which unfortunately has too frequently been one of circulation instead of reference. We have a number of men of wealth among us, any one or two of whom could confer upon their fellow-citizens no favor, nor secure for themselves more lasting honor, than by the judicious founding of a free public library.

The Lancasterian school system was established at Harrisburg by the act of the 11th April, 1827, and was abolished on the 20th of May, 1834, when the free or common schools went into operation. One need only take a survey of the magnificent school edifices, of the high standing of the teachers and the rapid advancement of the children, to fully realize the immense benefits derived from the Pennsylvania system of education. They need no encomium at our hands. The Harrisburg Academy established in 1809, is still in full vigor, and annually sends forth its young men prepared either for a higher collegiate course, or for the active pursuits of life.

The Harrisburg Bank was chartered on the 9th of May, 1814, with a capital of $300,000. William Wallace was its first President and John Downey, Cashier. It first went into operation at the then residence of its cashier in Second street, a few doors north-west of Cherry alley, where it remained until 1837, when the present site was purchased from the Bank of Philadelphia. At this time, in addition, eight banking institutions attend to the financial affairs of our community.

The removal of the seat of government to Harrisburg, although suggested as early as 1787, and often moved in the Assembly, did not prove successful until by the act of February, 1810, when "the offices of the State government were directed to be removed to the borough of Harrisburg, in the county of Dauphin," "within the month of October, 1812," and "the sessions of the Legislature thereafter there to be held." The first sessions of the Assembly were held in the court house, and that body continued to occupy the building until the completion of the Capitol.

No historical resume of Dauphin county can be called complete without some reference to the so-called "Buckshot War" of 1838. At the October election of that year David R. Porter, of Huntingdon, was chosen Governor, after a hotly contested political canvass, over Governor Ritner. The defeated party issued an ill-timed and ill-advised address, advising their friends "to treat the election as if it had not been held." It was determined, therefore, to investigate the election, and to do this the political complexion of the Legislature would be decisive. The majority of the Senate was Anti-Masonic, but the control of the House of Representatives hinged upon the admission of certain members from Philadelphia whose seats were contested. The votes of one of the districts in that city were thrown out by reason of fraud, and the Democratic delegation returned. The Anti-Masonic return judges refused to sign the certificates, "and both parties made out returns each for a different delegation, and sent them to the Secretary of the Commonwealth." The Democratic returns were correct, and should have been promptly received "without question."

When the Legislature met, the Senate organized by the choice of Anti-Masonic officers. In the House a fierce struggle ensued, both delegations claiming seats. The consequence was that each party went into an election for Speaker, each appointing tellers. Two Speakers were elected and took their seat upon the platform—William Hopkins being the choice of the Democrats, and Thomas S. Cunningham of the opposition. The Democrats believing that they were in the right, left out of view the rejection of the votes of the Philadelphia district. However, when the returns from the Secretary's office were opened, the certificate of the minority had been sent in, thus giving the advantage to the Anti-Masons. It was then a question which of the two Houses would be recognized by the Senate and the Governor.

At this stage of the proceedings, a number of men (from Philadelphia especially,) collected in the lobby, and when the Senate after organization proceeded to business, interrupted it by their disgraceful and menacing conduct. The other branch of the Legislature was in like manner disturbed, and thus both Houses were compelled to disperse. The crowd having taken possession of the halls proceeded to the court house, where impassioned harangues were indulged in and a committee of safety appointed. For several days all business was suspended and the Governor alarmed for his own personal safety, ordered out the militia, and fearing this might prove insufficient, called on the United States authorities for help. The latter refused, but the militia under Major Generals Patterson and Alexander, came promptly in response. For two or three days during this contest, the danger of a collision was imminent, but wiser counsels prevailed, and the Senate having voted to recognize the section of the House presided over by Mr. Hopkins, the so-called "Insurrection at Harrisburg" was virtually ended. This was what is commonly known as the "Buckshot War."

In the year 1860 Harrisburg received its highest corporate honors—that of a city. Although at the time arousing much opposition, yet its subsequent growth and prosperity have fully realized the fondest expectations of its earnest advocates. In population it ranks the sixth in the State, and in manufacturing interests it is the third—Pittsburgh and Philadelphia alone exceeding it—while in the Union it ranks high among the inland cities. As a native of the town we are proud of its prosperity, of its importance and its high social position.

It may not be out of place on this occasion to allude to the many citizens to whom this city and county of ours are indebted for their position, prominence and influence. Within the city's boundaries rest the remains of Governors Findley, Wolf, Porter and Geary. Honored and revered in the church were the Reverends Roan, Bartram, Sankey, Elder, Snodgrass, Snowden, Lochman, Castleman, Cookman, DeWitt, Winebrenner, Berg and Maher. Among the physicians were the Luthers, Agnew, Simonton, the Wiestlings, Fager, the Roberts, Reily, Dock, Orth, the Rutherfords, and the Seilers, with others celebrated in their day and generation. Of members of the bar, the names of Graydon, Patterson, Shunk, Douglass, McCormick, Elder, Fisher, Kunkel, Forster, M'Kinney, Wood, Alricks, Ayres, Rawn and Briggs present themselves. Of valued citizens, representative men, the Harrises, Maclays, Hanna, Hamilton, Berryhills, Wyeths, Hummel, Beatty, M'Clure, Buehlers, Espy, Sloan, Graydon, Downey, Shoch, Fleming, Bergner, Bombaugh, Kelker, Beader, Bucher, Cowden, M'Allister, Potts, Boyd, Kean, the Gilmores, Rutherfords, Grays, Allens, Haldemans, Elders, Cox, Ziegler, Forster, with hundreds of others, may be named—the worthy ancestors of prominent Dauphin county citizens of the present. In this Centennial anniversary let us do honor to their memories, recall their names, as we emulate their virtues.

Let us not forget on this occasion that within the limits of our county of Dauphin were born LINDLEY MURRAY the grammarian, WILLIAM DARBY the geographer, Rev. WILLIAM GRAHAM the founder of the now celebrated Washington and Lee University of Virginia, Commodore DAVID CONNOR, of the United States Navy, ALEXANDER M'NAIR, the first Governor of Missouri, with a long list of statesmen, divines and soldiers, representative men in the homes of their adoption—honored when living and revered while dead.

The townships of Peshtank, Lebanon and Derry covered the territory within the bounds of the counties of Dauphin and Lebanon in 1729, when Lancaster county was formed. From the time of the organization of the former county until 1813, when Lebanon was separated therefrom, the townships were as follows, with date of erection: Paxton, 1729; Lebanon, 1729; Derry, 1729; Hanover from Derry, 1737; Bethel from Lebanon, 1739; Heidelberg, 1757; Londonderry, 1768; Upper

Paxton, 1767; West Hanover, 1785; East Hanover, 1785; Middle Paxton, 1787; Swatara, 1799; Annville, 1799; Halifax, 1804, and Lykens, 1810. When Lebanon county was created, the townships of Lebanon, East and West Hanover, Heidelberg, Bethel and Annville were lost to Dauphin. Since that period there have been erected: Susquehanna, 1815; Mifflin, 1819; Rush, 1820; Jackson, 1828; Wiconisco, 1840; Lower Swatara, with new lines for Swatara, 1840; South, East and West Hanover, 1842; Jefferson, 1842; Washington, 1846; Reed, 1849; Conewago, 1850, and Williams, 1868.

The different boroughs and villages were laid out as follows: Harrisburg,1785; Middletown,1755; Hummelstown, 1762; Dauphin, 1826; Millersburg, 1807; Halifax, 1794; Gratz, 1805; Berrysburg, 1871; Lykens, 1847; Highspire, 1814; Linglestown,1765; Rockville,1839; Fisherville,1854; Wiconisco, 1848; Williamstown, 1869, and Uniontown, 1864. Many of these towns were settled years previously; but the plans were not officially recorded until the year noted.

At the time of the organization of the county of Dauphin, it contained a population of nearly 16,000, although in 1790, when the first census was taken, the number was only 18,177, due probably to the emigration of great numbers of the Scotch-Irish, who removed either westward or southward. In 1800—22,270. In 1810—31,-883. In 1820—21,653, a decrease, owing to the separation from it of the county of Lebanon, February 16, 1813, which by this census had a population of 16,975. In 1830—25,243. In 1840—30,118. In 1850—35,754. In 1860—46,756. In 1870—60,740. In 1876—at least 75,-000.

Of its 233,835 acres of land—61,249 acres, or almost one-fourth, is unimproved. The valuation of farm property, $20,000,000. As a farming community, however, Dauphin, owing to the large amount of untillable land, comes far down in the list of counties in the State. And yet the portion of the county lying between the Conewago hills and the Kittatinny mountains contains as highly cultivated and productive farms as any in the United States. Thrift and intelligence characterize the staid "Dutch" farmers of Dauphin, and they vie with any community in all that appertains to enterprise and progress. In manufacturing industries Dauphin is the sixth. Allegheny, Berks, Luzerne, Montgomery and Philadelphia alone surpassing her. The earliest industrial establishment in this locality was the "nailery" of Henry Fulton in 1785, although we must give precedence to the enterprise of the "noted Burney," who, five years previous, at his residence "in Upper Paxtang," manufactured counterfeit coin. His establishment was soon closed, however, the owner "sent to Lancaster goal," and, although "he left a great quantity of his cash in the hands of several," he never returned to claim it or renew the labors of his manufactory. Fulton's establishment was only a little remote from a "smithy." To look now at the industries of Harrisburg and the county of Dauphin, the progress within the last fifteen years is really wonderful, apart from the great contrast with fifty years ago. The number of manufactories of iron, alone, its furnaces, foundries, machine shops and nail works, form a list as gratifying to the citizens as it is surprising. The Pennsylvania steel works, the Lochiel iron works, M'Cormick's, Wister's, Dock's and Price's furnaces at Harrisburg, besides the Cameron at Middletown, one at Manada, and another near Dauphin. The Harrisburg Car and

Machine works, with a similar establishment at Middletown, Hickock's Eagle Works, Willson's, Jennings' and numberless other foundries scattered all over the county. These only represent the iron industries; time prevents an enumeration of the other sources of wealth. The coal mines of the Lykens Valley, with its boundless treasures, the development of the entire county by means of the various railroads projected or running through it, are designed to bring our county of Dauphin in the van of mineral wealth. The future will open up the riches hidden as yet from our view if the enterprise of its citizens but will it.

And now, fellow-citizens, in the hope that this brief historical record of the transactions of our locality may be acceptable to you and the people of my native town, county and State, I can only wish that in the coming hundred years their crowning glory may be the superior intelligence, the virtue and the integrity of their citizens, the love and loyalty of the people. Through Providence our fathers founded an empire great and grand. May their descendants, by the same benign and Divine influence, transmit the glorious heritage to the latest posterity.

www.ingramcontent.com/pod-product-compliance
Lightning Source LLC
Chambersburg PA
CBHW031443270326

41930CB00007B/849